Alma Lynne's

CROSS-STITCH *for* SPECIAL OCCASIONS

Dedication

With much love and devotion,
I dedicate this book to my mother, Elizabeth Stanton
Thompson, who taught me from birth, and
continues to remind me even now, that I can
accomplish anything if I do it with all my heart.
I love you, Mom.

In Gratitude

To Pam Swann,
my production manager, goes my
heartfelt gratitude for hours devoted above and
beyond the call of duty, and for delighting me time
and time again with her imaginative embellishments,
beautiful needlework, and fantastic attitude.
Thank you, good friend.

Library of Congress Catalog Number: 93-084607
ISBN: 0-8487-1121-1
Manufactured in the United States of America
First Printing 1993

Editor-in-Chief: Nancy J. Fitzpatrick
Senior Crafts Editor: Susan Ramey Wright
Senior Editor, Editorial Services:
Olivia Kindig Wells
Director of Manufacturing: Jerry Higdon
Art Director: James Boone

Alma Lynne's Cross-Stitch for Special Occasions

Editor: Laurie Pate Sewell
Assistant Editor: Shannon Leigh Sexton
Copy Chief: Mary Jean Haddin
Assistant Copy Editor: L. Amanda Owens
Copy Assistant: Leslee Rester Johnson
Production Manager: Rick Litton
Associate Production Manager: Theresa L. Beste
Production Assistant: Marianne Jordan
Designer: Diana Smith Morrison
Computer Artist: Karen Tindall Tillery
Photostylist: Katie Stoddard
Photographer: John O'Hagan
Senior Production Designer: Larry Hunter
Special Publishing Systems Administrator: Rick Tucker

Special Thanks

A special thank-you to Jim and Anne Smith
for the use of their beautiful home, to Martha
Knight for the use of her Christmas china, to Jody
and Robby Robinson for modeling our grandpar-
ents projects, and to Jim Green for his wonderful
floral arrangements.
Special help was provided by Geneal Rankin,
owner of Thread Bear in Birmingham, Alabama.
If you're ever in the area, stop by this cozy shop.
Alma Lynne Designs and Oxmoor House wish to
thank each of them for their time.

CONTENTS

WELCOME

On this beautiful spring morning, I sit by my kitchen window watching the flowers bloom and listening to the birds sing while my heart waits in anticipation for the release of my second hardcover book from Oxmoor House. Much thought and care went into creating tributes to occasions that have always been dear to my heart. I hope that you will also find these special and will be as eager as I was to make the first stitch towards cross-stitch treasures.

To appreciate handwork is to celebrate beauty in one of its most delicate forms. A masterpiece is created from a simple chart, a cutting of cloth, and a rainbow of threads. What a wonderful feeling to look upon your completed effort and know what all needleworkers know—a feeling of accomplishment and pride, the creation of something beautifully stitched by the hand and loved by the heart.

Celebrate life and love through cross-stitch sentiments handmade for yourself and others.

Your friend in cross-stitch,

Alma Lynne

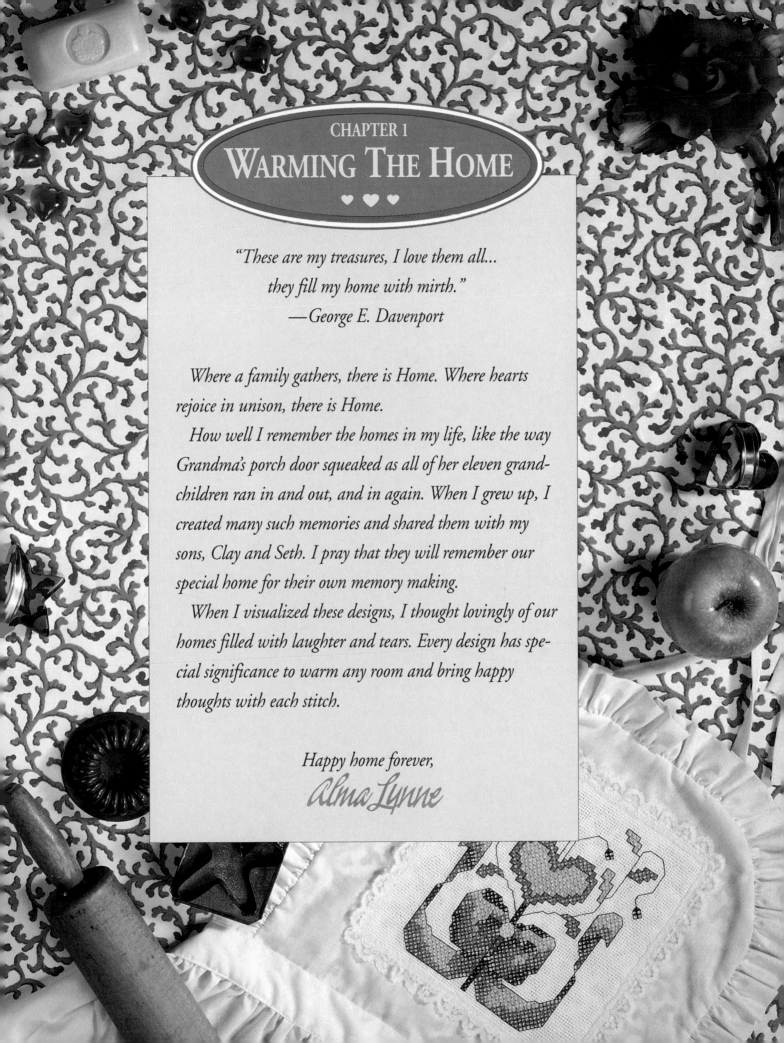

CHAPTER 1
WARMING THE HOME
♥ ♥ ♥

"These are my treasures, I love them all...
they fill my home with mirth."
—George E. Davenport

Where a family gathers, there is Home. Where hearts
rejoice in unison, there is Home.

How well I remember the homes in my life, like the way
Grandma's porch door squeaked as all of her eleven grand-
children ran in and out, and in again. When I grew up, I
created many such memories and shared them with my
sons, Clay and Seth. I pray that they will remember our
special home for their own memory making.

When I visualized these designs, I thought lovingly of our
homes filled with laughter and tears. Every design has spe-
cial significance to warm any room and bring happy
thoughts with each stitch.

Happy home forever,
Alma Lynne

Home Sampler

SAMPLE

Sample in photograph was stitched on cream 19-count Cork Linen over 2 threads. Design area is 12⅜" x 7⅜". Fabric was cut 19" x 14".

To personalize design, transfer desired letters and numbers from alphabet to graph paper, allowing 1 space between letters, 1 space between numbers, and 3 spaces between words. To determine center of name, count total number of spaces and divide by 2. Begin stitching center of name in center of area reserved for name in design. In same manner, center and stitch date below.

FABRICS	DESIGN AREAS
11-count	10¾" x 6⅜"
14-count	8⅜" x 5"
18-count	6½" x 3⅞"
22-count	5⅜" x 3⅛"

118
→ 70

MATERIALS

Completed cross-stitch on cream
  19-count Cork Linen; matching
  thread
¼ yard (45"-wide) blue pindot;
  matching thread
½ yard (45"-wide) rose fabric;
  matching thread
1¾ yard (¼") cording
1 (12½" x 23") piece of polyester
  fleece
Scrap of paperbacked fusible web
1 (20"-length) rose embroidery floss
Dressmaker's pen

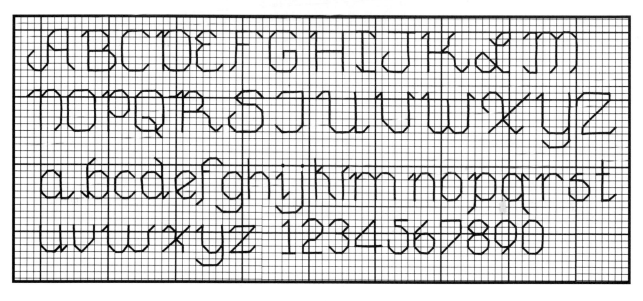

DMC Colors
(used for sample)
Step 1: Cross-stitch (2 strands)

`\`	`∠`	White
`^`	`⁄`	221 Shell Pink-vy. dk.
`I`		223 Shell Pink-med.
`C`	`⌐`	224 Shell Pink-lt.
`–`	`∕`	320 Pistachio Green-med.
`3`	`ℨ`	367 Pistachio Green-dk.
`\\`	`ⱶ`	839 Beige Brown-dk.
`つ`	`⌐`	840 Beige Brown-med.
`⁄⁄`	`⁄`	930 Antique Blue-dk.
`X`	`⁄`	931 Antique Blue-med.
`V`		932 Antique Blue-lt.
`O`	`⌐`	3721 Shell Pink-dk.
`⁄`		3750 Antique Blue-vy. dk.

Step 2: Backstitch (1 strand, except where noted)

931	Antique Blue-med. (2 strands) (date established)
3750	Antique Blue-vy. dk. (2 strands) (home name)
3371	Black Brown (all else)

HEART PATTERN

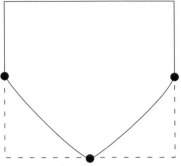

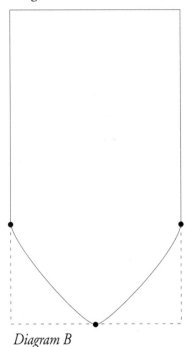

Diagram A

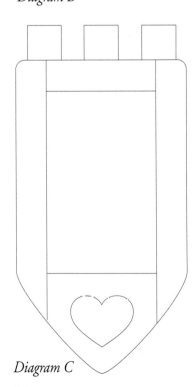

Diagram B

INSTRUCTIONS

All seam allowances are ¼".

1. With design centered, trim Cork Linen to 14" x 8½". From blue pindot, cut 1 (3" x 8½") strip for top border, 2 (3" x 18¾") strips for side borders, and 1 (8½" x 7¾") piece for bottom section. On 1 side border strip, measure and mark 3" from short bottom edge. Cut at an angle from bottom edge to mark. Repeat with remaining side border strip, marking and cutting on opposite side. On bottom section, find center and mark. From center point along bottom edge, measure and mark 5½" up each side edge. Cut at an angle from center mark to each side edge mark (see Diagram A). Also cut 3 (5½") squares for hanger loops.

From rose fabric, cut 1 (23½" x 13") piece for backing. On 1 short edge, find center and mark. From center point along bottom edge, measure and mark 8½" up each side edge. Cut at an angle from center mark to each side edge mark (see Diagram B). Also cut 1 (5") square for heart and 1"-wide bias strips, piecing as needed to equal 65". Make corded piping.

2. To make top of wall hanging: Use dressmaker's pen to mark center of each pindot border strip and center of each edge of design piece. With right sides facing, raw edges aligned, and center marks matching, sew top border strip to top of design piece, bottom section to bottom of piece, and side border strips to sides of piece (see Diagram C).

3. To make hanger loops, with right sides facing and raw edges aligned, fold each 5½" pindot square in half; stitch each along long raw edge. Trim edges and turn. Press strips flat and fold in half widthwise. On right side of design piece, with raw edges aligned, center and pin 1 loop along top edge; pin remaining loops approximately 1¼" from each side edge (see Diagram C). Baste in place.

4. To attach piping, with right sides facing and raw edges aligned, stitch piping to design piece, slightly rounding corners.

5. To attach heart, trace heart pattern on paper side of fusible web. Cut out just outside traced lines, leaving a margin. Fuse web to wrong side of 5" square of rose fabric. Cut out heart along traced lines. Peel off paper and center heart, fusible side down, on right side of bottom section of design piece (see Diagram C). Fuse heart in place. To embellish, make blanket stitches around edge of heart.

6. Baste fleece to wrong side of backing. With right sides facing, raw edges aligned, and loops toward center, stitch top to backing, sewing along stitching line of piping and enclosing hanger loops; leave opening for turning. Trim corners; turn. Slipstitch opening closed.

7. To make bows, cut rose floss into 4 (5") lengths. Referring to photograph, thread 1 length through each corner where design piece and pindot borders meet. Tie each in a bow.

Diagram C

Welcome

SAMPLE

Sample in photograph was stitched on ivory 28-count Annabelle over 2 threads. Design area is 1¼" x 4⅛". Fabric was cut 8" x 11".

Wooden frame (Stock No. 129-M) was supplied by Taylor's Workshop, 114 South Joyland Avenue, Durham, NC 27703.

FABRICS	DESIGN AREAS
11-count	1⅝" x 5⅜"
14-count	1¼" x 4¼"
18-count	1" x 3¼"
22-count	⅞" x 2⅝"

18
↑
→ 59

DMC Colors
(used for sample)

Step 1: Cross-stitch (2 strands)

/		221	Shell Pink-vy. dk.
V	⊿	223	Shell Pink-med.
C		224	Shell Pink-lt.
I	⊿	225	Shell Pink-vy. lt.
⟍	⊿	502	Blue Green
∧	⊿	503	Blue Green-med.
O		931	Antique Blue-med.
—		932	Antique Blue-lt.

Step 2: Backstitch (1 strand)

221	Shell Pink-vy. dk. (Welcome)
501	Blue Green-dk. (vine)

When Friends Gather

♥ ——————————

SAMPLE

Sample in photograph was stitched on ivory 14-count Aida over 2 threads. Design area is 19" x 16½". Fabric was cut 25" x 23".

FABRICS	DESIGN AREAS
11-count	12" x 10⅞"
14-count	9⅜" x 8½"
18-count	7⅜" x 6⅝"
22-count	6" x 5⅜"

132
↑
└→ 119

MATERIALS

Completed cross-stitch on ivory 14-count Aida; matching thread
1⅞ yards (45"-wide) green miniprint; matching thread
⅜ yard (45"-wide) green fabric
⅜ yard (45"-wide) pink fabric; matching thread
½ yard (45"-wide) pink-and-white stripe
1 (39½" x 37") piece of polyester fleece
3½ yards (⅛"-wide) white satin ribbon
3½ yards (⅛"-wide) pale pink satin ribbon
Dressmaker's pen

INSTRUCTIONS

All seam allowances are ¼".

1. With design centered, trim Aida to 21¼" x 18½". From mini-print, cut 1 (39½" x 37") piece for backing; cut 2 (28½" x 3½") strips and 2 (37½" x 3½") strips for border; also cut 5 (8½" x 3¼") strips for hanger loops. From green fabric, cut 2 (24¾" x 2¼") strips and 2 (18¾" x 2¼") strips for border. From pink fabric, cut 2 (39¾" x 1¾") strips and 2 (34¾" x 1¾") strips for border. From pink-and-white stripe, cut 2 (31¼" x 4") strips and 2 (21¾" x 4") strips for border.

2. To make top of wall hanging: Use dressmaker's pen to mark center of 1 long edge of each green border strip and center of each edge of design piece. With right sides facing, raw edges aligned, and center marks matching, sew short green strips to top and bottom of design piece and then long green strips to sides. In same manner: Mark and sew pink-and-white stripe border strips to green border strips; mark and sew miniprint border strips to pink-and-white stripe border strips; and mark and sew solid pink border strips to miniprint border strips.

3. To make hanger loops, with right sides facing and raw edges aligned, fold each miniprint strip in half lengthwise; stitch each along long raw edge. Trim edges and turn. Press strips flat and fold each in half widthwise. On right side of wall hanging, with raw edges aligned, center and pin 1 loop along top edge; pin 1 loop approximately ½" from each side; center and pin remaining loops between center loop and each side loop (see photograph).

4. Baste fleece to wrong side of backing. With right sides facing, raw edges aligned, and hanger loops toward center, stitch top to backing, enclosing hanger loops; leave an opening for turning. Trim corners and turn. Slipstitch opening closed.

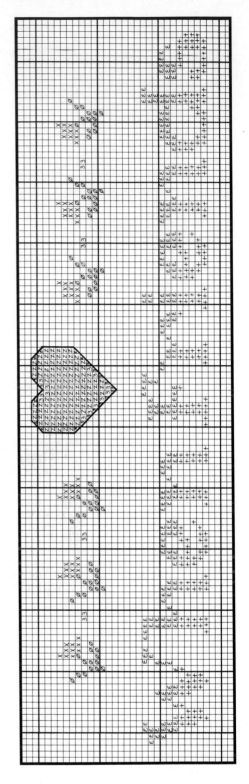

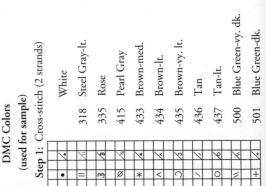

DMC Colors (used for sample)													
Step 1: Cross-stitch (2 strands)		White	318 Steel Gray-lt.	335 Rose	415 Pearl Gray	433 Brown-med.	434 Brown-lt.	435 Brown-vy. lt.	436 Tan	437 Tan-lt.	500 Blue Green-vy. dk.	501 Blue Green-dk.

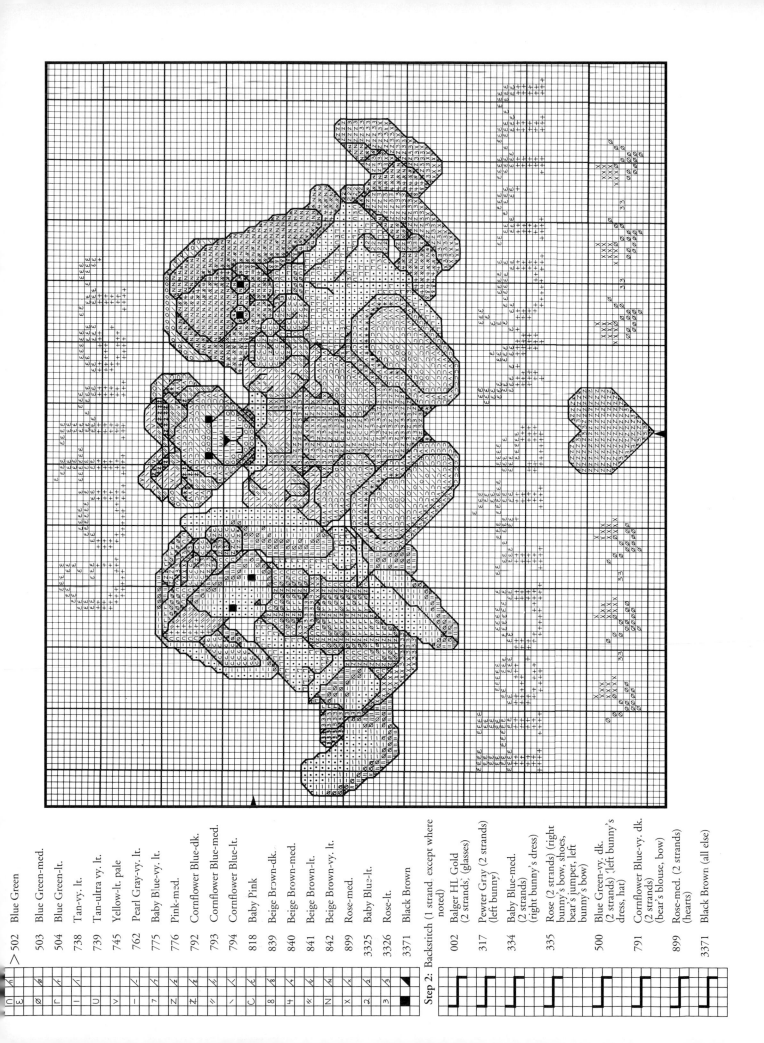

	502	Blue Green
	503	Blue Green-med.
	504	Blue Green-lt.
	738	Tan-vy. lt.
	739	Tan-ultra vy. lt.
	745	Yellow-lt. pale
	762	Pearl Gray-vy. lt.
	775	Baby Blue-vy. lt.
	776	Pink-med.
	792	Cornflower Blue-dk.
	793	Cornflower Blue-med.
	794	Cornflower Blue-lt.
	818	Baby Pink
	839	Beige Brown-dk.
	840	Beige Brown-med.
	841	Beige Brown-lt.
	842	Beige Brown-vy. lt.
	899	Rose-med.
	3325	Baby Blu-lt.
	3326	Rose-lt.
	3371	Black Brown

Step 2: Backstitch (1 strand, except where noted)

	002	Balger HL Gold (2 strands, (glasses))
	317	Pewter Gray (2 strands) (left bunny)
	334	Baby Blue-med. (2 strands) (right bunny's dress)
	335	Rose (2 strands) (right bunny's bow, shoes, bear's jumper, left bunny's bow)
	500	Blue Green-vy. dk. (2 strands) (left bunny's dress, hat)
	791	Cornflower Blue-vy. dk. (2 strands) (bear's blouse, bow)
	899	Rose-med. (2 strands) (hearts)
	3371	Black Brown (all else)

The Way to a Friend's House

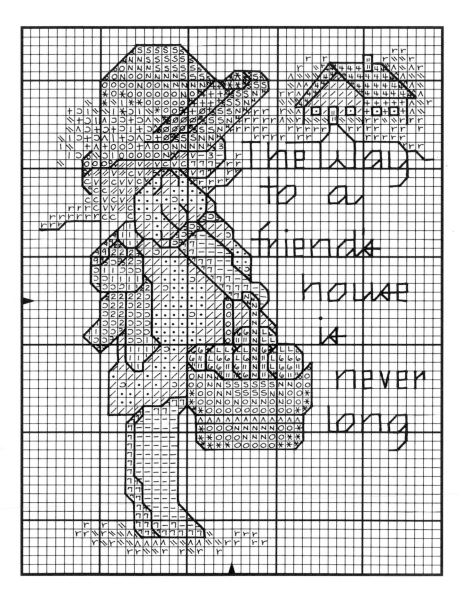

DMC Colors
(used for sample)

Step 1: Cross-stitch (2 strrands)

•	⁄.		White
∧	⁄	319	Pistachio Green-vy. dk.
∅	∅	334	Baby Blue-med.
3	3	353	Peach
\\	\\	367	Pistachio Green-dk.
⌐	⌐	368	Pistachio Green-lt.
*	*	435	Brown-vy. lt.
O	O	436	Tan
N	N	437	Tan-lt.
4	4	644	Beige Gray-med.
S	S	738	Tan-vy. lt.
7	7	754	Peach-lt.
6	6	760	Salmon
L	L	761	Salmon-lt.
/	/	775	Baby Blue-vy. lt.
ᴐ	ᴐ	776	Pink-med.
I	I	818	Baby Pink
9	9	899	Rose-med.
″	″	920	Copper-med.
V	V	921	Copper
C	C	922	Copper-lt.
–	–	948	Peach-vy. lt.
+	+	3325	Baby Blue-lt.
2	2	3326	Rose-lt.
II	III	3328	Salmon-dk.

Step 2: Backstitch (1 strand)

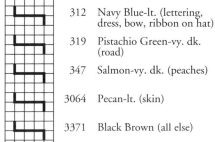

	312	Navy Blue-lt. (lettering, dress, bow, ribbon on hat)
	319	Pistachio Green-vy. dk. (road)
	347	Salmon-vy. dk. (peaches)
	3064	Pecan-lt. (skin)
	3371	Black Brown (all else)

SAMPLE

Sample in photograph was stitched on cream 18-count Tabby Cloth over 2 threads. Design area is 5" x 6½". Fabric was cut 11" x 13".

Candle screen (Stock No. 21001) was supplied by Sudberry House, P.O. Box 895, Old Lyme, CT 06371.

FABRICS
11-count
14-count
18-count
22-count

DESIGN AREAS
5¼" x 4⅛"
4⅛" x 3¼"
3¼" x 2½"
2⅝" x 2"

58
45

For Our Guest

SAMPLE

Sample in photograph was stitched on white 20-count Irish Linen over 2 threads. Design area is 2¾" x 6⅛". Fabric was cut 9" x 13".

Wooden towel rack (Stock No. 1320M) was supplied by Taylor's Workshop, 114 South Joyland Avenue, Durham, NC 27703.

FABRICS	DESIGN AREAS
11-count	2⅜" x 5½"
14-count	1⅞" x 4¼"
18-count	1½" x 3⅜"
22-count	1⅛" x 2¾"

DMC Colors
(used for sample)

Step 1: Cross-stitch (2 strands)

⁄	⁄	221	Shell Pink-vy. dk.
C	⁄	223	Shell Pink-med.
⁄	⁄	224	Shell Pink-lt.
ø	ø	502	Blue Green
X	⁄	3721	Shell Pink-dk.
^	⁄	3722	Shell Pink

Step 2: Backstitch (1 strand, except where noted)

	502	Blue Green (2 strands) (lettering)
	902	Garnet-vy. dk. (bow)

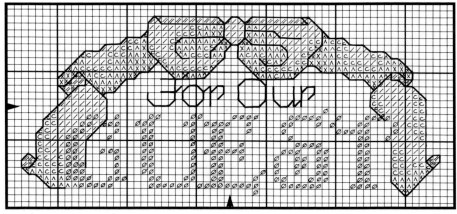

Home Is Where You Hang Stuff

SAMPLE

Sample in photograph was stitched on ivory 28-count Jubilee over 2 threads. Design area is 4" x 5⅝". Fabric was cut 10" x 12".

Pegged frame (Stock No. 136-M) was supplied by Taylor's Workshop, 114 South Joyland Avenue, Durham NC 27703.

FABRICS	DESIGN AREAS
11-count	5⅛" x 7⅛"
14-count	4" x 5⅝"
18-count	3⅛" x 4⅜"
22-count	2½" x 3½"

56
78

DMC Colors
(used for sample)

Step 1: Cross-stitch (2 strands)

V	⁄	221	Shell Pink-vy. dk.
∧	⁄	223	Shell Pink-med.
\	⁄	224	Shell Pink-lt.
–		225	Shell Pink-vy. lt.
I		930	Antique Blue-dk.
⁄		932	Antique Blue-lt.
C	⁄	3722	Shell Pink

Step 2: Backstitch (1 strand)

	902	Garnet-vy. dk. (bow)
	931	Antique Blue-med. (lettering)

Kitchen Cozies

♥ ─────────────

SAMPLES

Samples in photograph were stitched on white 14-count napkin, bread cover, and place mat over 1 thread and on purchased white 5½" x 8" x 15¾" toaster cover, 9" x 15½" x 8½" blender cover, 8¾" x 13½" x 14" mixer cover, and apron. A white 14-count Aida piece stitched over 2 threads was applied to each purchased item. Design areas are 3" x 2⅞" for napkin and bread cover, 1¾" x 5¾" for place mat, 3⅝" x 11⅛" for toaster cover, 10⅝" x 4¾" for blender cover, 8¼" x 7¾" for mixer cover, and 5¾" x 5⅝" for apron.

For napkin and bread cover, center design in 1 corner, leaving 7 threads unworked between bottom of design and corner, and 3 threads unworked on each adjacent side. For place mat, center design along edge of 1 long side, leaving 3 threads unworked below design.

For toaster cover, center design on Aida, leaving 2 threads unworked below design. Bind edges of a 5" x 12½" Aida piece and attach to center of cover front. For blender cover, center design on Aida, leaving 6 threads unworked below design. Bind edges of a 12½" x 5½" Aida piece and attach to center of cover front. For mixer cover, center design on Aida, leaving 3 threads unworked below design. Bind edges of a 9½" x 9¾" Aida piece and attach to cover front.

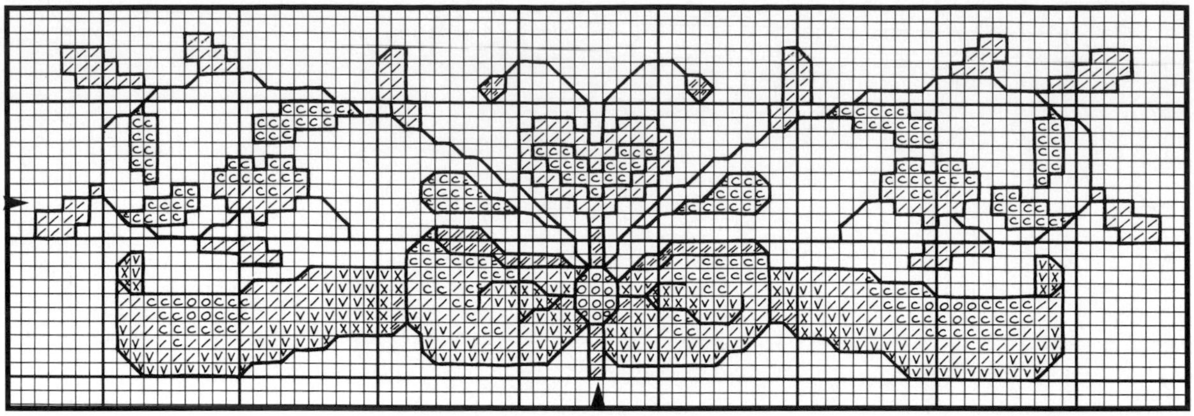

Place Mat and Toaster Cover

For apron, center design on Aida, leaving 3 threads unworked below design. Bind edges of a 7" x 7" Aida piece with lace attach to center of bib.

Napkin, bread cover, and place mat (Stock No. 1182) were supplied by Charles Craft, P.O. Box 1049, Laurinburg, NC 28352.

Note: *Samples in photograph were stitched on white with blue floss, but alternative colors may be substituted.*

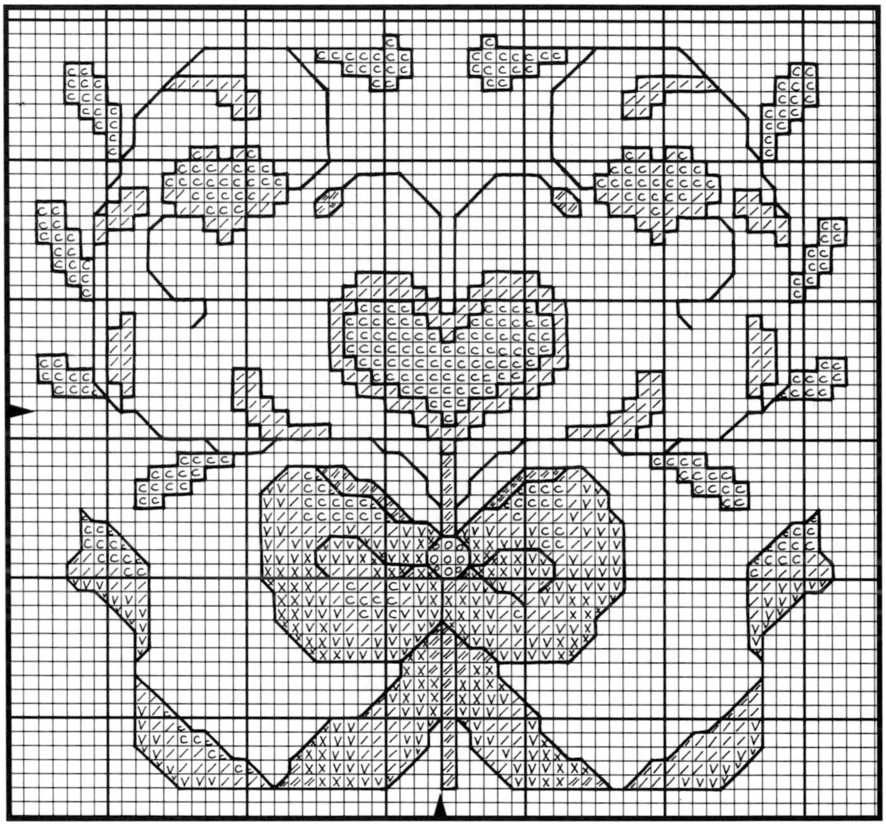

Mixer Cover

Place Mat and Toaster Cover

FABRICS	DESIGN AREAS
11-count	2¼" x 7⅜"
14-count	1¾" x 5¾"
18-count	1⅜" x 4½"
22-count	1⅛" x 3⅝"

25 ↑ → 81

Mixer Cover

FABRICS	DESIGN AREAS
11-count	5¼" x 4⅞"
14-count	4⅛" x 3⅞"
18-count	3¼" x 3"
22-count	2⅝" x 2½"

58 ↑ → 54

Napkin and Bread Cover

FABRICS	DESIGN AREAS
11-count	3⅞" x 3¾"
14-count	3" x 2⅞"
18-count	2⅜" x 2¼"
22-count	1⅞" x 1⅞"

42 ↑ → 41

Apron

FABRICS	DESIGN AREAS
11-count	3⅝" x 3½"
14-count	2⅞" x 2¾"
18-count	2¼" x 2⅛"
22-count	1⅞" x 1¾"

40 ↑ → 39

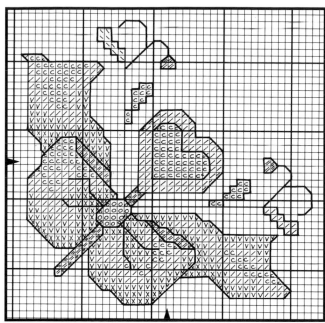

Napkin and Bread Cover

DMC Colors
(used for sample)

Step 1: Cross-stitch (2 strands)

⁄	⁄	311	Navy Blue-med.
X	x	312	Navy Blue-lt.
V	V	322	Navy Blue-vy. lt.
⁄	⁄	334	Baby Blue-med.
O	6	775	Baby Blue-vy. lt.
C	c	3325	Baby Blue-lt.

Step 2: Backstitch (1 strand)

⌐	311 Navy Blue-med.

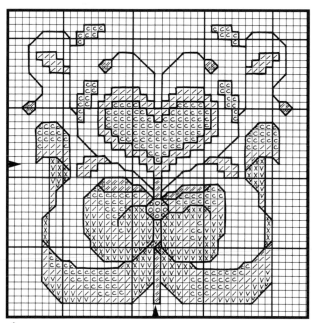

Apron

Blender Cover

FABRICS	DESIGN AREAS
11-count	6¾" x 3"
14-count	5¼" x 2⅜"
18-count	4⅛" x 1⅞"
22-count	3⅜" x 1½"

74

33

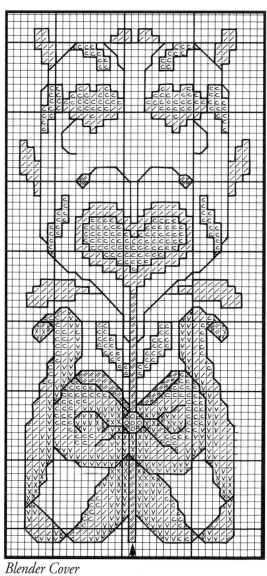

Blender Cover

25

Sewing Table and Pincushion

SAMPLES

Samples in photograph were stitched on cream 18-count Tabby Cloth over 2 threads for sewing table and on natural 28-count Linen over 2 threads for pincushion. Design areas are 8⅜" x 5⅞" for sewing table and 5⅜" x 3¾" for pincushion. Fabric was cut 15" x 12" for sewing table and 12" x 10" for pincushion.

Sewing table (Stock No. 4745-PF) was supplied by Sudberry House, P.O. Box 895, Old Lyme, CT 06371. Mount cross-stitch according to manufacturer's instructions.

FABRICS	DESIGN AREAS
11-count	6⅞" x 4¾"
14-count	5⅜" x 3¾"
18-count	4⅛" x 3"
22-count	3⅜" x 2⅜"

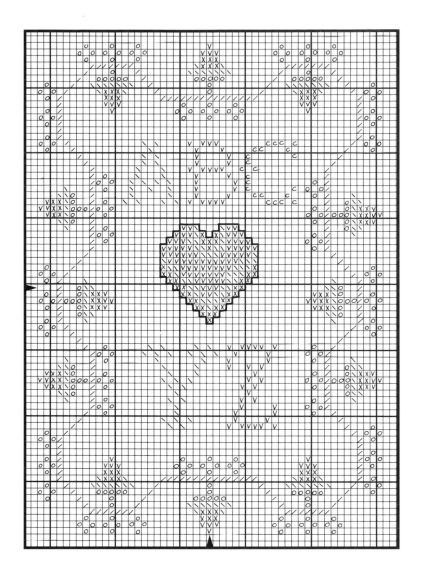

DMC Colors
(used for sample)

Step 1: Cross-stitch (2 strands)

＼	223	Shell Pink-med.
v	224	Shell Pink-lt.
C	225	Shell Pink-vy. lt.
／	502	Blue Green
O	503	Blue Green-med.
X	3722	Shell Pink

Step 2: Backstitch (1 strand)

	221	Shell Pink-vy. dk.

MATERIALS (for pincushion)

Completed cross-stitch on natural 28-count Linen; matching thread
¼ yard (45"-wide) rose fabric; matching thread
¾ yard (¼") cording
Stuffing

INSTRUCTIONS

All seam allowances are ¼".

1. With design centered, trim Linen to 6½" x 5". From rose fabric, cut 1 (6½" x 5") piece for back; also cut 1"-wide bias strips, piecing as needed to equal 21". Make corded piping.

2. With right sides facing and raw edges aligned, stitch piping to design piece, slightly rounding corners. With right sides facing, raw edges aligned, and piping toward center, stitch design piece to back, sewing along stitching line of piping and leaving an opening for turning. Trim corners; turn and stuff firmly. Slipstitch opening closed.

A country chair in the window there
Holds my favorite teddy bear
And on a quilt from Mama's bed,
I dream of bedtime stories read
Oh, how I love to reminisce
Of Mama's sweet, endearing kiss.

To Somebunny Special

One day you came into my w
My darling little baby girl
And every   day my ble
Mount to   numbers m
Too great   to count.
I'm thankful
Everyday   for you
Be with   May God
I pray   you dear

Love, Mom

CHAPTER 2
SPECIAL PEOPLE
★ ★ ★

"And the song from beginning to end,
I found again in the heart of a friend."
— Henry Wadsworth Longfellow

To love and to be loved is life's sweetest blessing. I believe paths cross not by coincidence but as part of a divine plan. And each person that crosses our path has a gift to offer. Celebrate those special people who bring light into your life with a labor-of-love gift—one that touches the heart. What a personal way to say I love you.

I hope the offerings in this chapter will speak of lovely things to you and yours.

Celebrate special people,

Alma Lynne

To Somebunny Special

SAMPLE

Sample in photograph was stitched on daffodil 28-count Pastel Linen over 2 threads. Design area is 6⅝" x 4½". Fabric was cut 13"x 11".

FABRICS	DESIGN AREAS
11-count	8⅜" x 5¾"
14-count	6⅝" x 4⅝"
18-count	5⅛" x 3½"
22-count	4⅛" x 2⅞"

92

64

MATERIALS

Completed cross-stitch on daffodil 28-count Pastel Linen; matching thread
⅝ yard (45"-wide) green fabric; matching thread
¼ yard (45"-wide) light pink fabric; matching thread
⅓ yard (45"-wide) green miniprint
1¼ yard (2½"-wide) scalloped antique white lace edging
1 (15¾" x 13¼") piece of polyester fleece
1⅞ yard (1"-wide) pink grosgrain ribbon
Dressmaker's pen
2 (1"-wide) plastic loops

INSTRUCTIONS

All seam allowances are ¼".

1. With design centered, trim Pastel Linen to 8" x 5¾". From green fabric, cut 1 (15½" x 13¼") piece for backing; also cut 2 (9½" x 1¼") strips and 2 (5½" x 1¼") strips for border. From light pink fabric, cut 2 (12⅛" x 1⅞") strips and 2 (10" x 2") strips for border. From miniprint, cut 2 (15½" x 2¼") strips and 2 (9½" x 2¼") strips for border. From lace, cut 2 (12⅛") strips and 2 (10") strips.

2. To make top of wall hanging: Use dressmaker's pen to mark center of 1 long edge of each green border strip and center of each edge of design piece. With right sides facing, raw edges aligned, and center marks matching, sew short green border strips to top and bottom of design piece and then long green border strips to sides. In same manner: Mark and sew light pink border strips to green border strips; mark and sew lace strips over light pink border strips; and mark and sew miniprint border strips to light pink-and-lace border strips.

3. Baste fleece to wrong side of backing. With right sides facing and raw edges aligned, stitch top to backing, leaving an opening for turning. Trim corners and turn. Slipstitch opening closed.

4. Cut pink ribbon into 4 (16") strips. Tie each length into a bow. Referring to photograph, tack 1 bow to each corner where lace edging meets miniprint.

5. On backing, slipstitch 1 plastic hanging loop 1½" from top and 3½" from each side.

To Somebunny Special

DMC Colors
(used for sample)

Step 1: Cross-stitch (2 strands)

−	∕	White
∅	⟋	500 Blue Green-vy. dk.
Z	⟋	502 Blue Green
∧	⟋	503 Blue Green-med.
C	⟋	504 Blue Green-lt.
7	⟋	776 Pink-med.
I	⟋	818 Baby Pink

⟍	⟋	838 Beige Brown-vy. dk.
V	⟋	839 Beige Brown-dk.
∕	⟋	840 Beige Brown-med.
S	⟋	841 Beige Brown-lt.
O	⟋	842 Beige Brown-vy. lt.
e	⟋	899 Rose-med.
3	⟋	3326 Rose-lt.
■		3371 Black Brown

Step 2: Backstitch (1 strand)

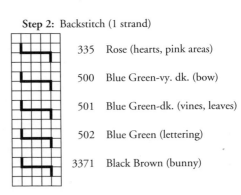

335 Rose (hearts, pink areas)

500 Blue Green-vy. dk. (bow)

501 Blue Green-dk. (vines, leaves)

502 Blue Green (lettering)

3371 Black Brown (bunny)

Chance Made Us Sisters

SAMPLE

Sample in photograph was stitched on lavender 18-count Davosa over 2 threads. Design area is 13½" x 7¼". Fabric was cut 20" x 13¼".

FABRICS	DESIGN AREAS
11-count	11⅜" x 5⅞"
14-count	8⅞" x 4⅝"
18-count	7" x 3⅝"
22-count	5⅝" x 3"

125

65

MATERIALS

Completed cross-stitch on lavender 18-count Davosa; matching thread

⅔ yard (45"-wide) lavender fabric

¼ yard (45"-wide) pink fabric; matching thread

¼ yard (45"-wide) green fabric; matching thread

⅓ yard (45"-wide) white-and-lavender miniprint; matching thread

1 (25½" x 18¾") piece of polyester fleece

2⅜ yards (⅜"-wide) white satin ribbon

2⅜ yards (⅜"-wide) lavender satin ribbon

1 yard (¼"-wide) pink satin ribbon

⅝ yard (⅛"-wide) lavender satin ribbon

Dressmaker's pen

2 (1"-wide) plastic loops

INSTRUCTIONS

All seam allowances are ¼".

1. With design centered, trim Davosa to 15" x 8½". From lavender fabric, cut 1 (25½" x 18¾") piece for backing; also cut 2 (25½" x 1¼") strips and 2 (19" x 1¼") strips for border. From pink fabric, cut 2 (16½" x 1¼") strips and 2 (8½" x 1¼") strips for border. From green fabric, cut 2 (19½" x 2") strips and 2 (10" x 2") strips for border. From miniprint, cut 2 (24⅛" x 3") strips and 2 (17½" x 3") strips for border.

2. To make top of wall hanging: Use dressmaker's pen to mark center of 1 long edge of each pink border strip and center of each edge of design piece. With right sides facing, raw edges aligned, and center marks matching, sew short pink border strips to top and bottom of design piece and then long pink border strips to sides. In same manner: Mark and sew green border strips to pink border strips; mark and sew miniprint border strips to green border strips; and mark and sew lavender border strips to miniprint border strips.

3. Baste fleece to wrong side of backing. With right sides facing and raw edges aligned, stitch top to backing, leaving an opening for turning. Trim corners and turn. Slipstitch opening closed.

4. Cut ⅜"-wide white and lavender ribbons into 3 (17") lengths each. Handling 1 length of each as 1, tie into a bow. Repeat to make 3 bows; set aside. From remaining ⅜"-wide ribbons, cut 2 pieces each in various lengths; cut pink ribbon in half. Handling all lengths as 1, tie into a large bow. Tie ⅛"-wide lavender ribbon into a knot around center of large bow to secure. Tack to upper right corner where green and miniprint borders meet. Tack remaining bows to remaining corners in same manner. Trim ends of ribbons at an angle.

5. On backing, slipstitch 1 loop 2" from top and 3" from each side.

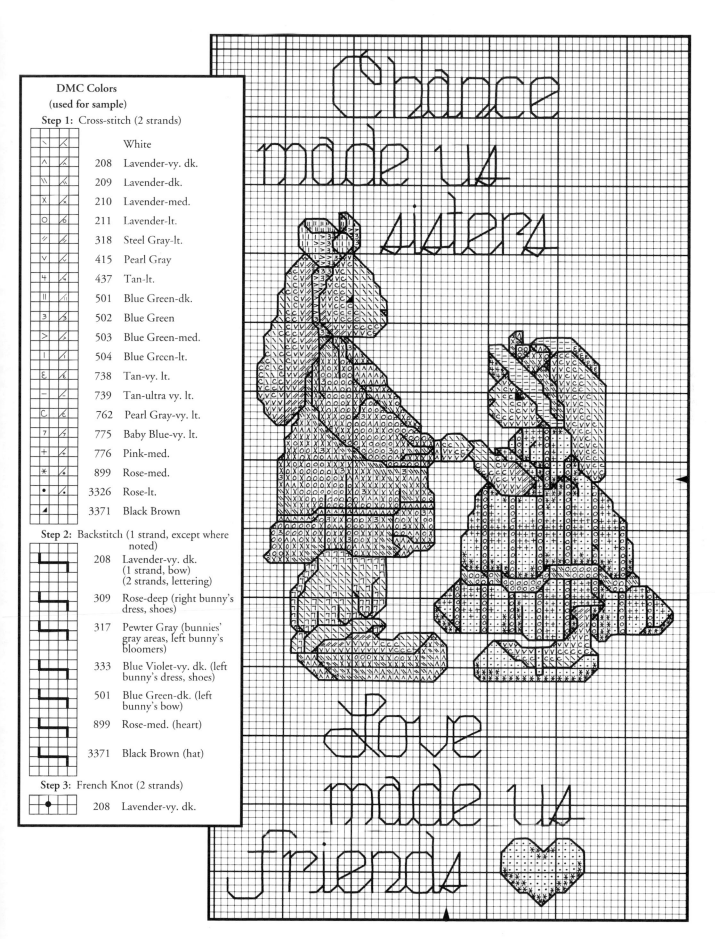

DMC Colors
(used for sample)

Step 1: Cross-stitch (2 strands)

⟍ ⟋		White
∧	208	Lavender-vy. dk.
⟍⟍	209	Lavender-dk.
X	210	Lavender-med.
O	211	Lavender-lt.
⟋⟋	318	Steel Gray-lt.
V	415	Pearl Gray
4	437	Tan-lt.
‖	501	Blue Green-dk.
3	502	Blue Green
>	503	Blue Green-med.
	504	Blue Green-lt.
ε	738	Tan-vy. lt.
−	739	Tan-ultra vy. lt.
C	762	Pearl Gray-vy. lt.
7	775	Baby Blue-vy. lt.
+	776	Pink-med.
∗	899	Rose-med.
•	3326	Rose-lt.
◢	3371	Black Brown

Step 2: Backstitch (1 strand, except where noted)

	208	Lavender-vy. dk. (1 strand, bow) (2 strands, lettering)
	309	Rose-deep (right bunny's dress, shoes)
	317	Pewter Gray (bunnies' gray areas, left bunny's bloomers)
	333	Blue Violet-vy. dk. (left bunny's dress, shoes)
	501	Blue Green-dk. (left bunny's bow)
	899	Rose-med. (heart)
	3371	Black Brown (hat)

Step 3: French Knot (2 strands)

●	208	Lavender-vy. dk.

35

A Special Brother

SAMPLE

Sample in photograph was stitched on natural 19-count Highland over 2 threads. Design area is 7¾" x 5¼". Fabric was cut 14" x 12".

FABRICS	DESIGN AREAS
11-count	6¾" x 4½"
14-count	5¼" x 3½"
18-count	4⅛" x 2¾"
22-count	3⅜" x 2¼"

74

49

DMC Colors
(used for sample)

Step 1: Cross-stitch (2 strands)

−			White
II		318	Steel Gray-lt.
v		319	Pistachio Green-vy. dk.
X		355	Terra Cotta-dk.
I		356	Terra Cotta-med.
C		367	Pistachio Green-dk.
*		433	Brown-med.
4		434	Brown-lt.
<		435	Brown-vy. lt.
3		436	Tan
ε		437	Tan-lt.
7		762	Pearl Gray-vy. lt.
8		801	Coffee Brown-dk.
⁄		890	Pistachio Green-ultra dk.
\\		930	Antique Blue-dk.
^		931	Antique Blue-med.
•		932	Antique Blue-lt.
z		3023	Brown Gray-lt.
⊃		3024	Brown Gray-vy. lt.
ø		3371	Black Brown

Step 2: Backstitch (1 strand, except where noted)

890	Pistachio Green-ultra dk. (2 strands)
3371	Black Brown (all else)

Step 3: French Knot (2 strands)

3371	Black Brown (eye)

MATERIALS

Completed cross-stitch on natural 19-count Highland; matching thread
¼ yard (45"-wide) brown fabric; matching thread
½ yard (45"-wide) hunter green pindot; matching thread
1½ yards (¼") cording
¾ yard (⅝"-wide) medium green grosgrain ribbon; matching thread
½ yard (½"-wide) light blue grosgrain ribbon; matching thread
½ yard (1"-wide) hunter green grosgrain ribbon
1 (10" x 13") piece of polyester batting
1 (12") bellpull hanger rod
Dressmaker's pen
Fabric glue

INSTRUCTIONS

All seam allowances are ¼".

1. With design centered, trim Highland to 9¼" x 6¾". From brown fabric, cut 2 (2⅝" x 6¾") strips and 2 (2½" x 13½") strips for border. From pindot, cut 1 (10¾" x 13½") piece for backing; also cut 1"-wide bias strips, piecing as needed to equal 48". Make corded piping. From medium green ribbon, cut 2 (7") strips and 2 (4") strips. From light blue ribbon, cut 2 (5") strips and 2 (4") strips. From hunter green ribbon, cut 4 (4") strips.

2. To make top of wall hanging: Use dressmaker's pen to mark center of 1 long edge of brown border strips and center of each edge of design piece. With right sides facing, raw edges aligned, and center marks matching, first sew short brown border strips to top and bottom of design piece and then long brown border strips to sides.

3. Referring to photograph, glue 1 (7") medium green ribbon, 1 (5") light blue ribbon, and 1 hunter green ribbon to top left corner of design piece. Trim ends of ribbons to match sides. Repeat to attach ribbons in bottom right corner (see photograph).

4. To make hanger loops, refer to photograph and glue 1 color each of remaining 4" strips to a scrap of brown fabric. Trim excess fabric, if necessary. Fold in half to form loop. Repeat for second loop. Set aside.

5. To attach piping, with right sides facing and raw edges aligned, stitch piping to design piece, slightly rounding corners.

6. Baste fleece to wrong side of backing. With raw edges aligned, pin hanger loops to top of design piece, approximately 1¾" from each side edge. With right sides facing, raw edges aligned, and loops toward center, stitch top to backing along stitching line of piping, enclosing loops and leaving an opening for turning. Trim corners; turn. Slipstitch opening closed. Insert bellpull rod through hanger loops.

Memories of Mama & Papa

A country chair in the window there
Holds my favorite teddy bear
And on a quilt from Mama's bed,
I dream of bedtime stories read
Oh, how I love to reminisce
Of Mama's sweet, endearing kiss.

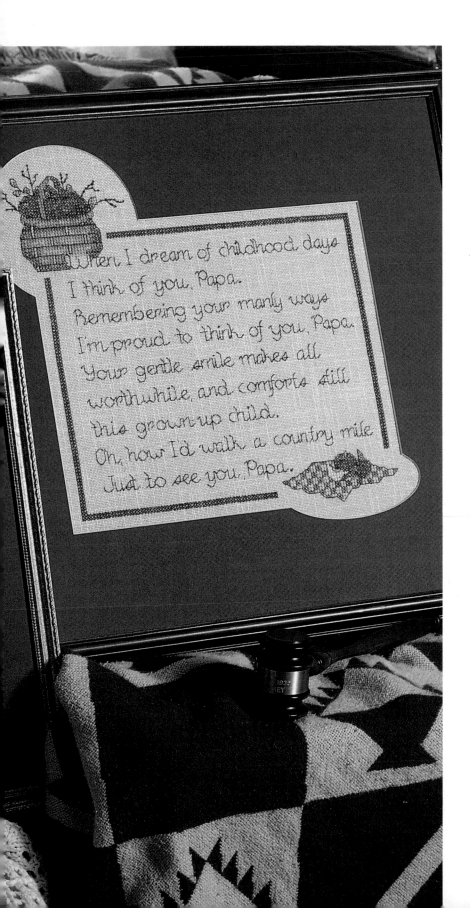

SAMPLES

Samples in photograph were stitched on white 20-count Ariosa over 2 threads for Mama and on camel 18-count Highland over 2 threads for Papa. Design areas are 10½" x 14" for Mama and 13¼" x 13⅞" for Papa. Fabric was cut 17" x 20" for Mama and 19¼" x 20" for Papa.

Mama Poem

FABRICS	DESIGN AREAS
11-count	9⅛" x 12¼"
14-count	7⅛" x 9⅝"
18-count	5½" x 7½"
22-count	4½" x 6⅛"

100
↓
└→ 135

Papa Poem

FABRICS	DESIGN AREAS
11-count	10⅞" x 11⅜"
14-count	8½" x 8⅞"
18-count	6⅝" x 7"
22-count	5⅜" x 5⅝"

119
↑
└→ 125

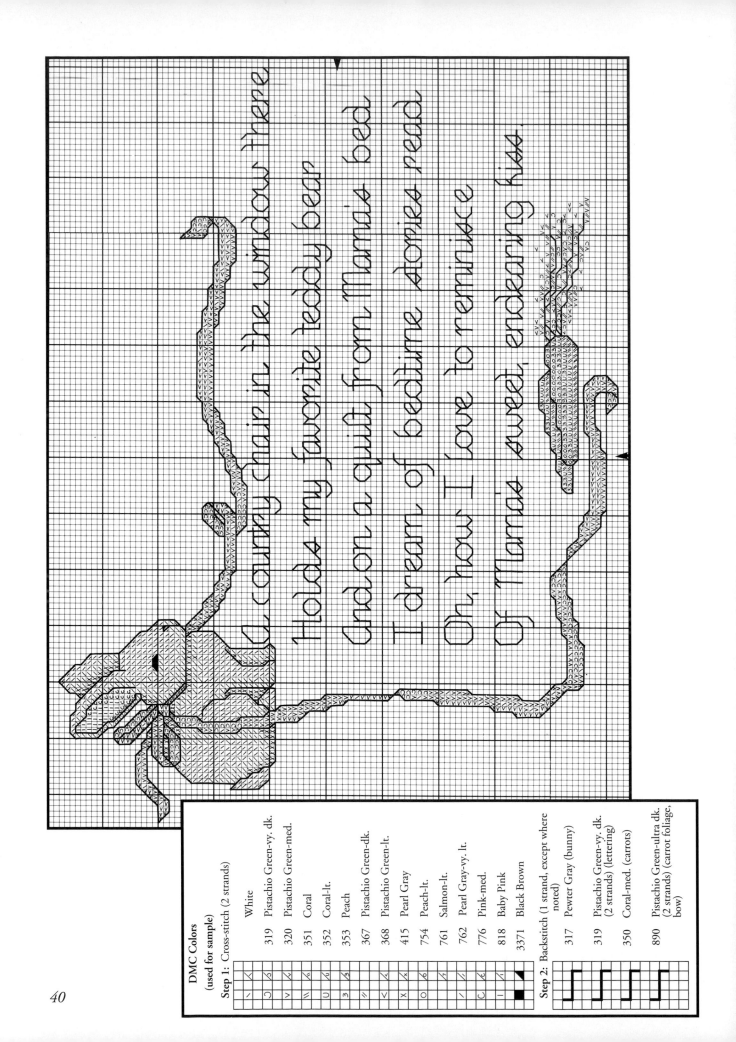

A country chair in the window there,
Holds my favorite teddy bear
And on a quilt from Mama's bed
I dream of bedtime stories read
Oh, how I love to reminisce
Of Mama's sweet, endearing kiss.

DMC Colors
(used for sample)

Step 1: Cross-stitch (2 strands)

/		White
X	319	Pistachio Green–vy. dk.
C	320	Pistachio Green–med.
>	351	Coral
=	352	Coral–lt.
U	353	Peach
3	367	Pistachio Green–dk.
%	368	Pistachio Green–lt.
<	415	Pearl Gray
X	754	Peach–lt.
O	761	Salmon–lt.
/	762	Pearl Gray–vy. lt.
C	776	Pink–med.
I	818	Baby Pink
◣	3371	Black Brown

Step 2: Backstitch (1 strand, except where noted)

	317	Pewter Gray (bunny)
	319	Pistachio Green–vy. dk. (2 strands) (lettering)
	350	Coral–med. (carrots)
	890	Pistachio Green–ultra dk. (2 strands) (carrot foliage, bow)

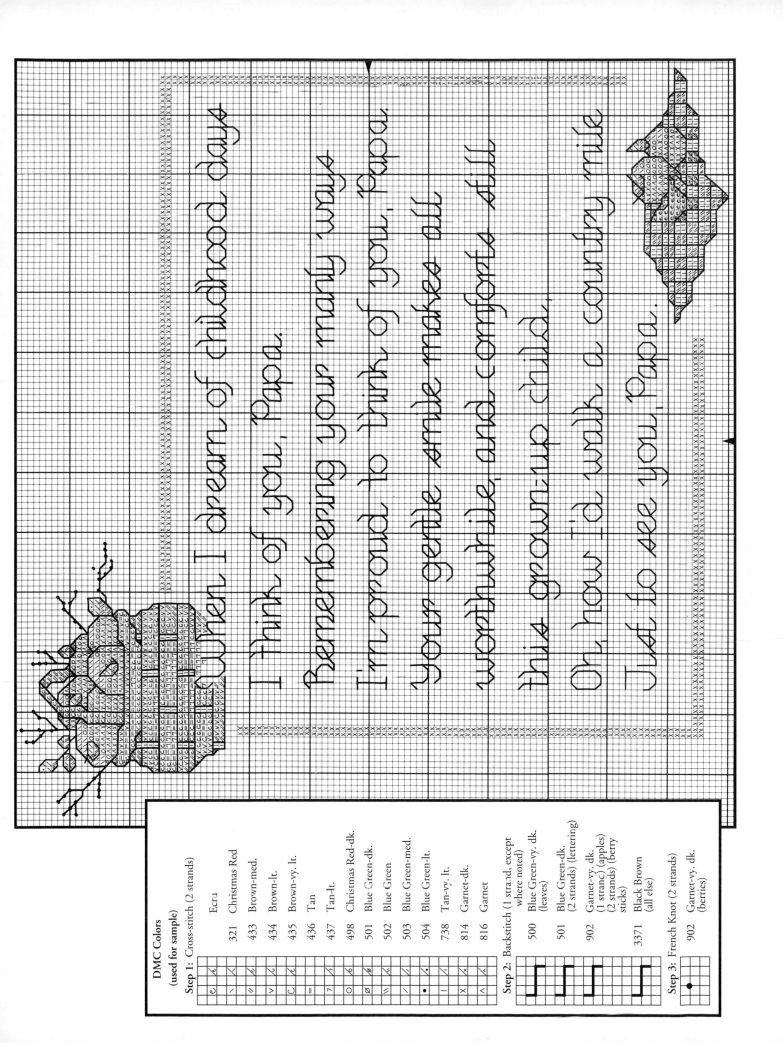

When I dream of childhood days

I think of you, Papa.

Remembering your manly ways

I'm proud to think of you, Papa.

Your gentle smile makes all

worthwhile and comforts all

this grown-up child,

Oh how I'd walk a country mile

Just to see you, Papa.

DMC Colors
(used for sample)

Step 1: Cross-stitch (2 strands)

e		Ecru
/	321	Christmas Red
X	433	Brown-med.
∕	434	Brown-lt.
V	435	Brown-vy. lt.
C	436	Tan
=	437	Tan-lt.
7	498	Christmas Red-dk.
O	501	Blue Green-dk.
Ø	502	Blue Green
II	503	Blue Green-med.
∕	504	Blue Green-lt.
•	738	Tan-vy. lt.
I	814	Garnet-dk.
X	816	Garnet
∧		

Step 2: Backstitch (1 strand, except where noted)

	500	Blue Green-vy. dk. (leaves)
	501	Blue Green-dk. (2 strands) (lettering)
	902	Garnet-vy. dk. (1 strand) (apples) (2 strands) (berry sticks)
	3371	Black Brown (all else)

Step 3: French Knot (2 strands)

•	902	Garnet-vy. dk. (berries)

To My Husband

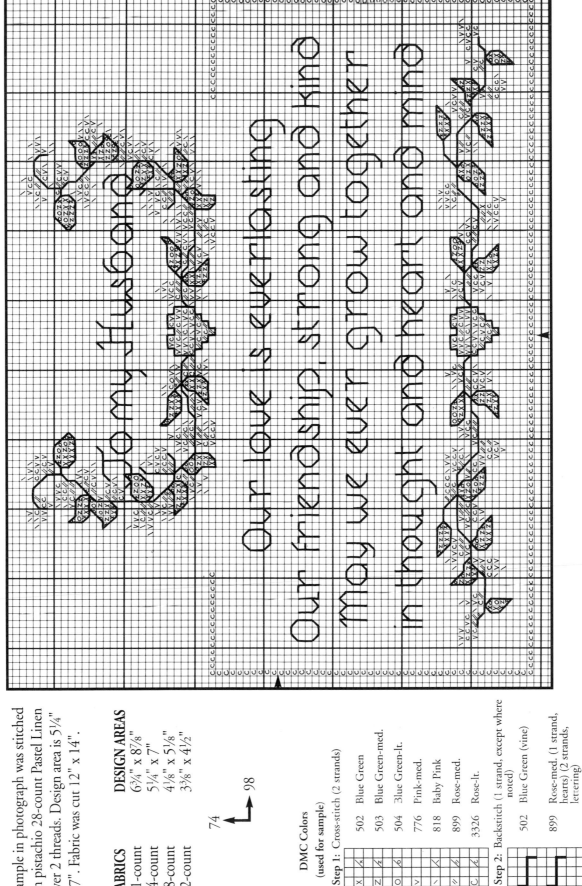

SAMPLE

Sample in photograph was stitched on pistachio 28-count Pastel Linen over 2 threads. Design area is 5¼" x 7". Fabric was cut 12" x 14".

FABRICS	DESIGN AREAS
11-count	6¾" x 8⅞"
14-count	5¼" x 7"
18-count	4⅛" x 5⅝"
22-count	3⅜" x 4½"

74
98

DMC Colors
(used for sample)

Step 1: Cross-stitch (2 strands)

x	X	502	Blue Green
z	Z	503	Blue Green-med.
O	O	504	Blue Green-lt.
v	V	776	Pink-med.
/	X	818	Baby Pink
//	Z	899	Rose-med.
C	Z	3326	Rose-lt.

Step 2: Backstitch (1 strand, except where noted)

502 Blue Green (vine)

899 Rose-med. (1 strand, hearts) (2 strands, lettering)

43

My Baby Girl

★ ─────────────────────────────────────

SAMPLE

Sample in photograph was stitched on ivory 28-count Annabelle over 2 threads. Design area is 5½" x 7". Fabric was cut 12" x 13".

FABRICS	DESIGN AREAS
11-count	8⅛" x 9⅛"
14-count	6⅜" x 7⅛"
18-count	5" x 5½"
22-count	4" x 4½"

89
↓→ 100

44

One day you came into my world
My darling little baby girl.
And every day my blessings
Mount to numbers much
Too great to count.
I'm thankful for you
Every day... May God
Be with you dear.
I pray. Love, Mom

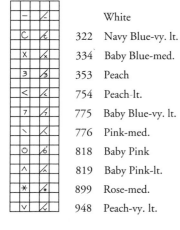

DMC Colors
(used for sample)

Step 1: Cross-stitch (2 strands)

− /		White
C ¢	322	Navy Blue-vy. lt.
X ✗	334	Baby Blue-med.
3 ʒ	353	Peach
< ∠	754	Peach-lt.
7 ⁊	775	Baby Blue-vy. lt.
\ ╲	776	Pink-med.
O ◔	818	Baby Pink
∧ ⋀	819	Baby Pink-lt.
* ✶	899	Rose-med.
V ⋁	948	Peach-vy. lt.

/ /	3325	Baby Blue-lt.
⫽ ⫽	3326	Rose-lt.

Step 2: Backstitch (1 strand)

312 Navy Blue-lt.
322 Navy Blue-vy. lt.
334 Baby Blue-med.
(lettering in alternating colors in this order 312, 322, 334)

312 Navy Blue-lt. (shoes, dress)

334 Baby Blue-med. (bonnet, sleeves, bloomers)

500 Blue Green-vy. dk. (flower stems)

758 Terra Cotta-lt. (skin)

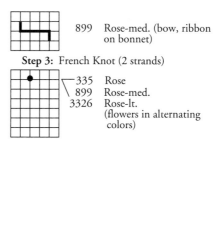

899 Rose-med. (bow, ribbon on bonnet)

Step 3: French Knot (2 strands)

• 335 Rose
899 Rose-med.
3326 Rose-lt.
(flowers in alternating colors)

My Baby Son

★ ──

SAMPLE

Sample in photograph was stitched
on ivory 28-count Annabelle over 2
threads. Design area is 6⅞" x 7⅜".
Fabric was cut 13" x 14".

FABRICS	DESIGN AREAS
11-count	8¾" x 9⅜"
14-count	6⅞" x 7⅜"
18-count	5⅜" x 5¾"
22-count	4⅜" x 4⅝"

96

103

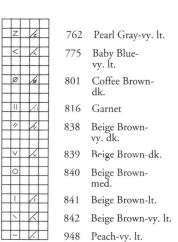

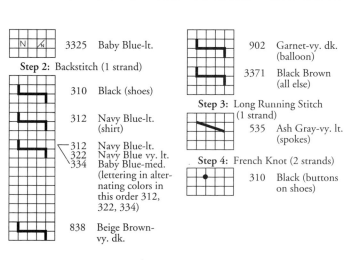

DMC Colors
(used for sample)

Step 1: Cross-stitch (2 strands)

		White
•	310	Black
∧	318	Steel Gray-lt.
3	353	Peach
\\	413	Pewter Gray-dk.
X	414	Steel Gray-dk.
C	415	Pearl Gray
4	498	Christmas Red-dk.
⊘	535	Ash Gray-vy. lt.
7	754	Peach-lt.

Z	762	Pearl Gray-vy. lt.
<	775	Baby Blue-vy. lt.
∅	801	Coffee Brown-dk.
II	816	Garnet
//	838	Beige Brown-vy. dk.
V	839	Beige Brown-dk.
O	840	Beige Brown-med.
I	841	Beige Brown-lt.
\	842	Beige Brown-vy. lt.
−	948	Peach-vy. lt.

N	3325	Baby Blue-lt.

Step 2: Backstitch (1 strand)

310 Black (shoes)

312 Navy Blue-lt. (shirt)

312 Navy Blue-lt.
322 Navy Blue vy. lt.
334 Baby Blue-med. (lettering in alternating colors in this order 312, 322, 334)

838 Beige Brown-vy. dk.

902 Garnet-vy. dk. (balloon)

3371 Black Brown (all else)

Step 3: Long Running Stitch (1 strand)

535 Ash Gray-vy. lt. (spokes)

Step 4: French Knot (2 strands)

310 Black (buttons on shoes)

#1 Grandparents

Samples in photograph were stitched on white 14-count sweatshirt over 1 thread for All-American Grandma and on white 14-count cap over 1 thread for #1 Grandpa. Design areas are 3⅞" x 13¾" for All-American Grandma and 3" x 7" for #1 Grandpa. Center designs in fabric areas and begin stitching.

Sweatshirt (Stock No. 990-6066) was supplied by Janlynn Corporation, 34 Front Street, Indian Orchard, MA 01151.

Cap (Stock No. 10650) was supplied by Daniel Enterprises, 5521 Scotch Meadows Drive, Laurinburg, NC 28352.

All-American Grandma

FABRICS	DESIGN AREAS
11-count	4⅞" x 17½"
14-count	3⅞" x 13¾"
18-count	3" x 10⅝"
22-count	2½" x 8¾"

54
↑
└→ 192

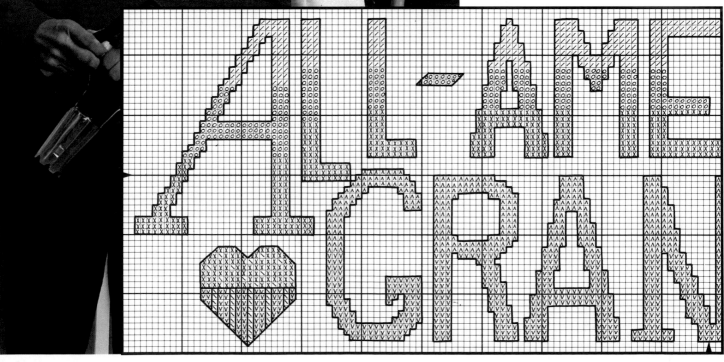

Step 1: Cross-stitch (2 strands)

` `		`/`		White
`∧`				498 Christmas Red-dk.
`∨`		`/`		814 Garnet-dk.
`X`		`/`		930 Antique Blue-dk.
`O`		`6`		931 Antique Blue-med.
`/`				932 Antique Blue-lt.

Step 2: Backstitch (1 strand)

3371   Black Brown

#1 Grandpa

FABRICS	DESIGN AREAS
11-count	3¾" x 8⅝"
14-count	2⅞" x 6¾"
18-count	2¼" x 5¼"
22-count	1⅞" x 4⅜"

41

95

DMC Colors
(used for sample)

Step 1: Cross-stitch (2 strands)

`O`				White
`//`				814 Garnet-dk.
`X`		`/`		930 Antique Blue-dk.
`I`				931 Antique Blue-med.
`/`				932 Antique Blue-lt.

Step 2: Backstitch (1 strand)

3371   Black Brown

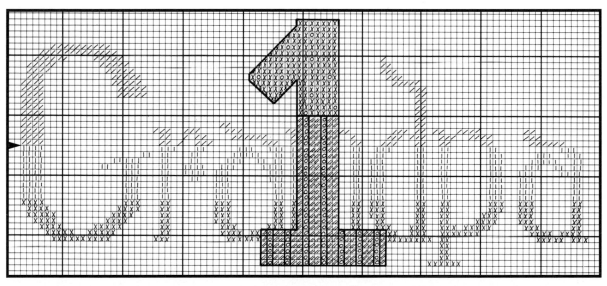

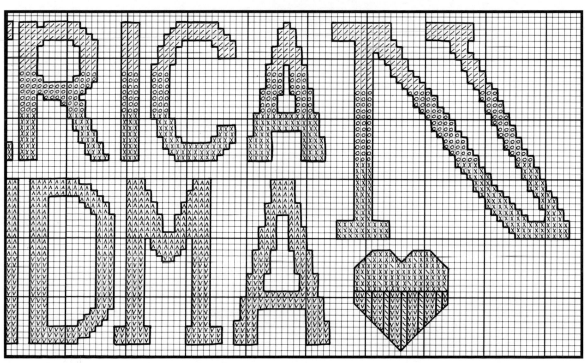

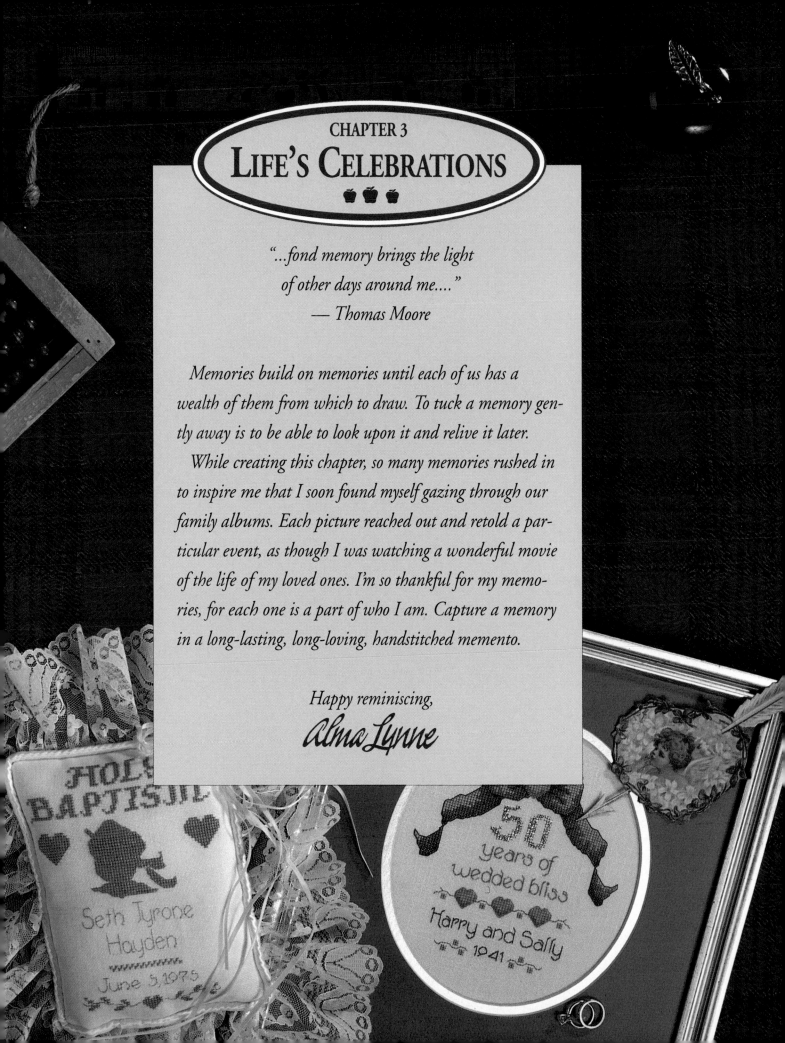

CHAPTER 3
LIFE'S CELEBRATIONS

*"...fond memory brings the light
of other days around me...."*
— Thomas Moore

*Memories build on memories until each of us has a
wealth of them from which to draw. To tuck a memory gen-
tly away is to be able to look upon it and relive it later.*

*While creating this chapter, so many memories rushed in
to inspire me that I soon found myself gazing through our
family albums. Each picture reached out and retold a particular event, as though I was watching a wonderful movie
of the life of my loved ones. I'm so thankful for my memories, for each one is a part of who I am. Capture a memory
in a long-lasting, long-loving, handstitched memento.*

Happy reminiscing,

Alma Lynne

HOLY
BAPTISM

Seth Tyrone
Hayden

June 5, 1975

50
years of
wedded bliss

Harry and Sally
1941

Holy Baptism Pillows

SAMPLES

Samples in photograph were stitched on white 28-count Quaker Cloth over 2 threads. Design area is 7¼" x 5" for each. Fabric was cut 14" x 11" for each.

To personalize design, transfer desired letters and numbers from alphabet to graph paper, allowing 3 spaces between words. To determine center of name, count total number of spaces and divide by 2. Begin stitching center of name in center of of area reserved for name in design. In same manner, center and stitch date below.

Note: Center and stitch boy or girl between hearts, as shown by arrows on chart.

FABRICS	DESIGN AREAS
11-count	8⅝" x 6⅜"
14-count	6¾" x 5"
18-count	5¼" x 3⅞"
22-count	4⅜" x 3⅛"

95

70

MATERIALS (for 1 pillow)

Completed cross-stitch on white 28-count Quaker Cloth; matching thread
⅜ yard (45"-wide) white satin
¾ yard (¼") cording
1½ yards (3½"-wide) white lace edging
3⅝ yards (⅛"-wide) white satin ribbon
Small ribbon rosette in desired color
Polyester fiberfill

INSTRUCTIONS

All seam allowances are ¼".

1. With design centered, trim Quaker Cloth to 8½" x 6¾". From white satin, cut 1 (8½" x 6¾") piece for pillow back; also cut ½"-wide bias strips, piecing as needed to equal 29". Make corded piping.

2. To attach piping, with right sides facing and raw edges aligned, stitch piping to design piece, slightly rounding corners.

3. To attach lace, run gathering threads along bound edge of lace. With right sides facing and gathered edge of lace aligned with raw edges of design piece, pin lace to design piece, gathering to fit. Stitch along stitching line of piping, through all layers.

4. With right sides facing, raw edges aligned, and piping and lace toward center, stitch pillow front to back, leaving an opening for turning. Trim corners; turn and stuff firmly. Slipstitch opening closed.

5. Cut satin ribbon into 5 (26") lengths. Handling all lengths as 1, tie into a bow. Referring to photograph, tack bow to top right corner and tack rosette in center of bow.

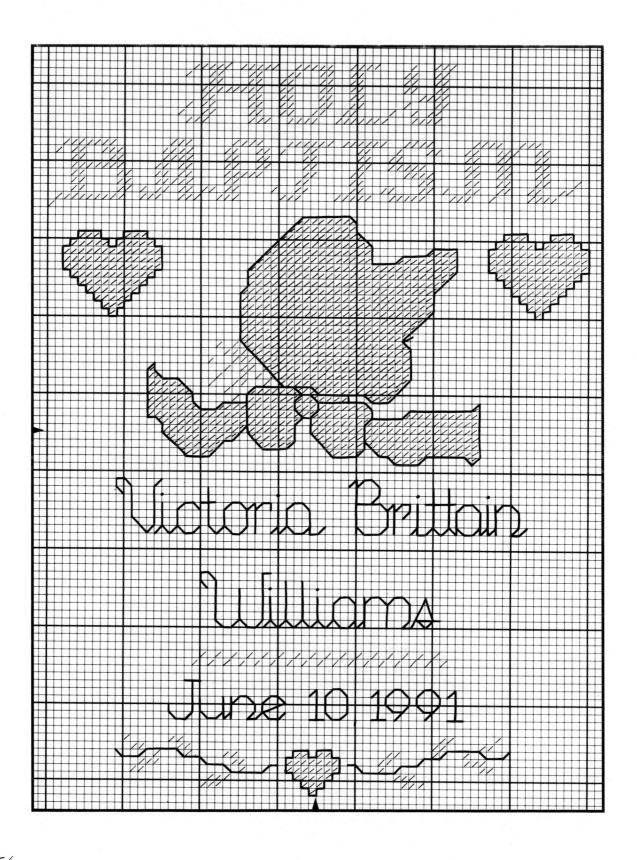

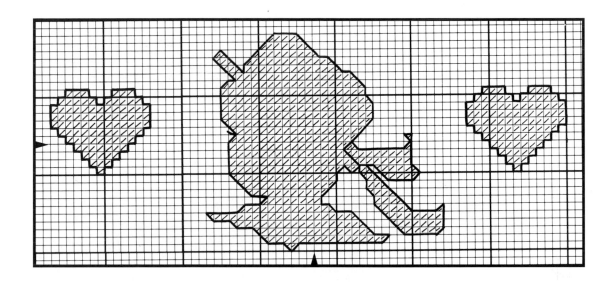

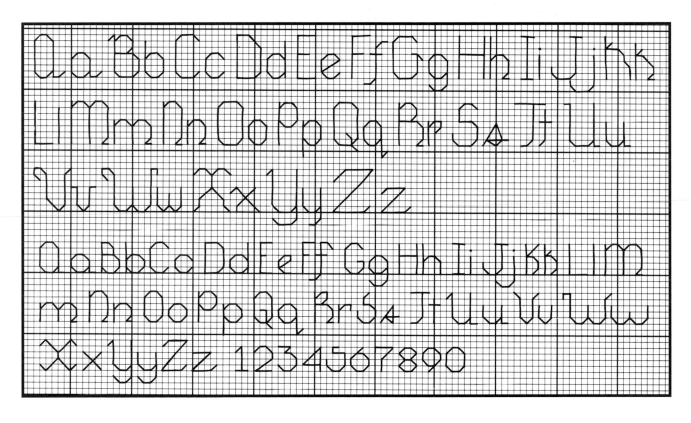

DMC Colors
(used for sample)
Step 1: Cross-stitch (2 strands)

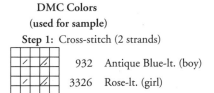

932   Antique Blue-lt. (boy)

3326   Rose-lt. (girl)

Step 2: Backstitch (1 strand)

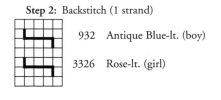

932   Antique Blue-lt. (boy)

3326   Rose-lt. (girl)

First Day of School

SAMPLE

Sample in photograph was stitched on tea-dyed 28-count Linen over 2 threads. Design area is 7¼" x 4⅛". Fabric was cut 14" x 11".

To personalize design, transfer desired letters from alphabet to graph paper. Refer to graph for correct spacing between each letter, number, and word. To determine center for name, count total number of spaces and divide by 2. Begin stitching center of name in center of area reserved for name in design. In same manner, center and stitch date in space reserved for date in design.

FABRICS	DESIGN AREAS
11-count	9¼" x 5¼"
14-count	7¼" x 4⅛"
18-count	5⅝" x 3¼"
22-count	4⅝" x 2⅝"

102
↑
→ 58

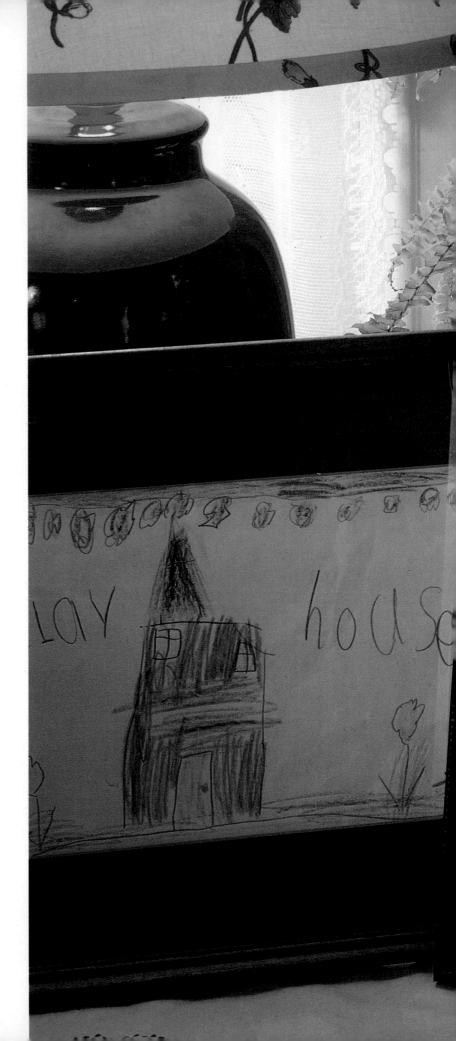

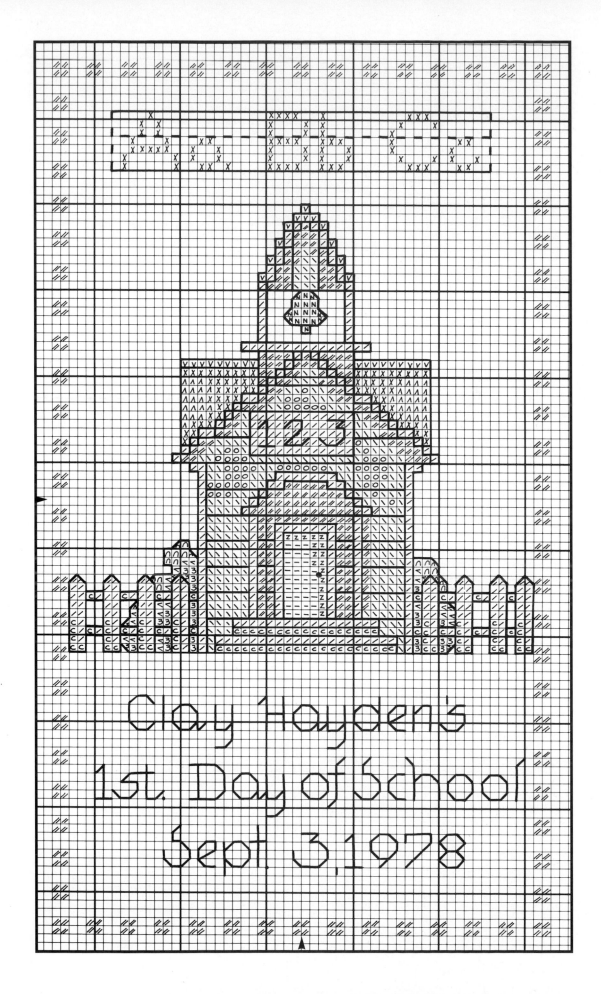

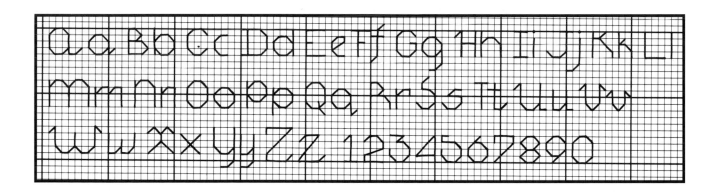

DMC Colors

(used for sample)

Step 1: Cross-stitch (2 strands)

✓	⁄		White
⁄⁄		221	Shell Pink-vy. dk.
<	∠	320	Pistachio Green-med.
3	ℨ	367	Pistachio Green-dk.
∩	⋔	368	Pistachio Green-lt.
Z		642	Beige Gray-dk.
−		644	Beige Gray-med.
C		762	Pearl Gray-vy. lt.
X		930	Antique Blue-dk.
∧	⋏	931	Antique Blue-med.
V		3371	Black Brown
╲		3721	Shell Pink-dk.
O		3722	Shell Pink
N	⋈	002	Balger HL Gold

Step 2: Backstitch (1 strand, except where noted)

221	Shell Pink-vy. dk. (2 strands) (lettering)
890	Pistachio Green-ultra dk. (greenery)
3371	Black Brown (school, fence, writing lines)

Step 3: French Knot (1 strand)

●	3371 Black Brown

For My Teacher

SAMPLES

Samples in photograph were stitched on white 19-count Cork Linen over 2 threads for basket label and apple pin and on white 18-count lace jar top over 2 threads. Design areas are 3¼" x 9" for basket label, 2" x 2" for apple pin, and 1¼" x 1¼" for lace jar top. Fabric was cut 10" x 15" for basket label and 6" x 6" for apple pin.

For lace jar top, center and stitch 1 apple motif on fabric, leaving ⅞" unworked on all sides.

Lace jar top (Stock No. 2-24) was supplied by Tish and Amy Originals, P.O. Box 514, Centreville, AL 35042.

Note: Use alphabet from "First Day of School," page 59, for personalization.

Basket Label

FABRICS	DESIGN AREAS
11-count	2⅞" x 7¾"
14-count	2¼" x 6⅛"
18-count	1¾" x 4¾"
22-count	1⅜" x 3⅞"

31
↑
↳ 85

Apple Pin

FABRICS	DESIGN AREAS
11-count	2¼" x 2¼"
14-count	1¾" x 1¾"
18-count	1⅜" x 1⅜"
22-count	1⅛" x 1⅛"

25
↑
↳ 25

DMC Colors
(used for sample)

Step 1: Cross-stitch (2 strands)

I		320	Pistachio Green-med.
O	6	321	Christmas Red
3	3	367	Pistachio Green-dk.
/	/	498	Christmas Red-dk.
X	X	814	Garnet-dk.
^	^	815	Garnet-med.
C	C	816	Garnet
//	//	902	Garnet-vy. dk.

Step 2: Backstitch (1 strand)

	890	Pistachio Green-ultra dk. (leaves)
	3371	Black Brown (apples, stems, lettering)

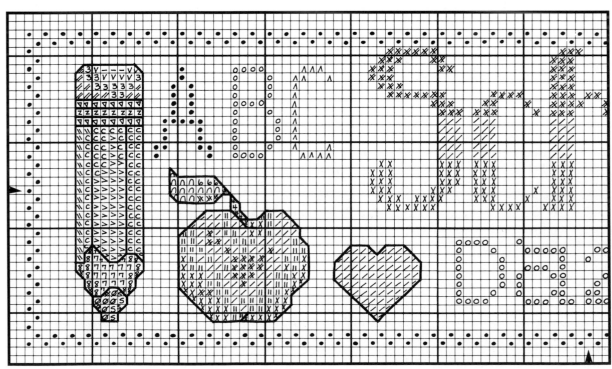

Book Bag

SAMPLE

Sample in photograph was stitched on cream 14-count book bag over 1 thread. Center design in fabric area and begin stitching. Embellish straps with bows as desired.

Book bag (Stock No. 961-101) was supplied by Janlynn Corporation, 34 Front Street, Indian Orchard, MA 01151.

FABRICS / DESIGN AREAS

FABRICS	DESIGN AREAS
11-count	3⅜" x 11⅞"
14-count	2⅝" x 9⅜"
18-count	2" x 7¼"
22-count	1⅝" x 6"

37 ↑
→ 131

DMC Colors
(used for sample)

Step 1: Cross-stitch (2 strands)

●	311	Navy Blue-med.
O	312	Navy Blue-lt.
Ø	317	Pewter Gray
∩	320	Pistachio Green-med.
✶	321	Christmas Red
∧	322	Navy Blue-vy. lt.
U	334	Baby Blue-med.
⁄⁄	352	Coral-lt.
3	353	Peach
✗	367	Pistachio Green-dk.
6	368	Pistachio Green-lt.
S	414	Steel Gray-dk.
Z	415	Pearl Gray
4	433	Brown-med.
⁄	498	Christmas Red-dk.
＼＼	725	Topaz
C	726	Topaz-lt.
>	727	Topaz-vy. lt.
8	738	Tan-vy. lt.
7	739	Tan-ultra vy. lt.
V	754	Peach-lt.
▽	762	Pearl Gray-vy. lt.
X	814	Garnet-dk.
II	815	Garnet-med.
—	948	Peach-vy. lt.
P	3325	Baby Blue-lt.

Step 2: Backstitch (1 strand)

⌐	3371	Black Brown

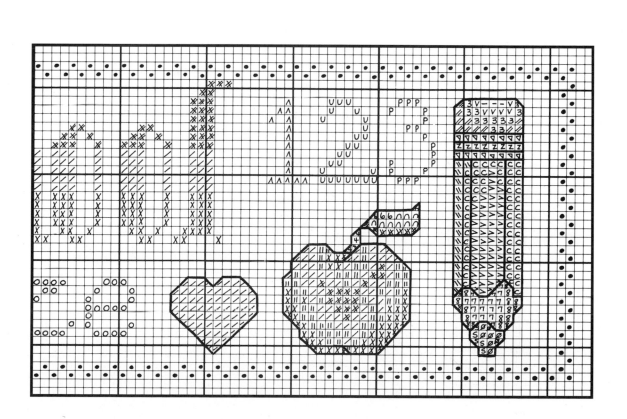

Congratulations, Graduate!

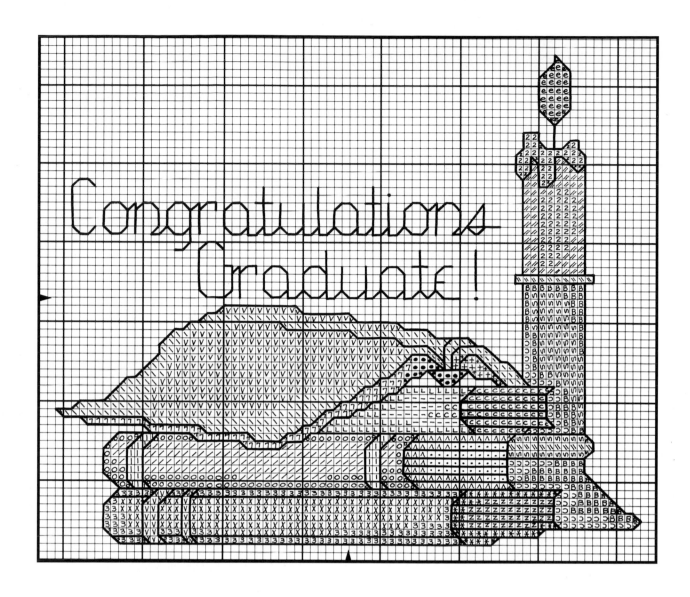

SAMPLE

Sample in photograph was stitched on cream 18-count Tabby Cloth over 2 threads. Design area is 7⅜" x 8½". Fabric was cut 14" x 15".

FABRICS	DESIGN AREAS
11-count	5⅝" x 6¾"
14-count	4½" x 5¼"
18-count	3½" x 4⅛"
22-count	2⅞" x 3⅜"

62
74

DMC Colors
(used for sample)

Step 1: Cross-stitch (2 strands)

v	⟋		White
X	⟋	311	Navy Blue-med.
+	⟋	318	Steel Gray-lt.
o	⟋	319	Pistachio Green-vy. dk.
3	⟋	336	Navy Blue
/	⟋	367	Pistachio Green-dk.
B	⟋	436 002	Tan Balger HL Gold (2 strands)
c	⟋	437 002	Tan-lt. Balger HL Gold (2 strands)
*	⟋	644	Beige Gray-med.
7	⟋	725	Topaz
e	⟋	726	Topaz-lt.
⌐	⟋	738 002	Tan-vy. lt. Balger HL Gold (2 strands)
∧	⟋	738	Tan-vy. lt.

\\	⟋	739 002	Tan-ultra vy. lt. Balger HL Gold (2 strands)
•		739	Tan-ultra vy. lt.
L	⟋	743	Yellow-med.
–	–	744	Yellow-pale
C	⟋	745	Yellow-lt. pale
\	⟋	762	Pearl Gray-vy. lt.
•	⟋	783	Christmas Gold
Z		822	Beige Gray-lt.
⫽	⟋	827	Blue-vy. lt.
2	⟋	828	Blue-ultra vy. lt.

Step 2: Backstitch (1 strand, except where noted)

⌐	336	Navy Blue (lettering) (2 strands)
	3371	Black Brown (all else)

You're Looking at a Graduate

SAMPLE

Sample in photograph was stitched on cream 28-count Pastel Linen over 2 threads. Design area is 4⅝" x 6¾". Fabric was cut 11" x 13".

Gold mirror (Stock No. 2207-G) was supplied by Sudberry House, P.O. Box 895, Old Lyme, CT 06371.

FABRICS	DESIGN AREAS
11-count	5⅞" x 8⅝"
14-count	4⅝" x 6¾"
18-count	3⅝" x 5¼"
22-count	3" x 4⅜"

DMC Colors
(used for sample)

Step 1: Cross-stitch (2 strands)

\\	223	Shell Pink-med.
O	224	Shell Pink-lt.
X	319	Pistachio Green-vy. dk.
>	320	Pistachio Green-med.
C	367	Pistachio Green-dk.
/	368	Pistachio Green-lt.
v	890	Pistachio Green-ultra dk.
x	3722	Shell Pink

Step 2: Backstitch (1 strand, except where noted)

	221	Shell Pink-vy. dk. (tulips)
	890	Pistachio Green-ultra dk. (stems, leaves)
	3722	Shell Pink (2 strands) (lettering)

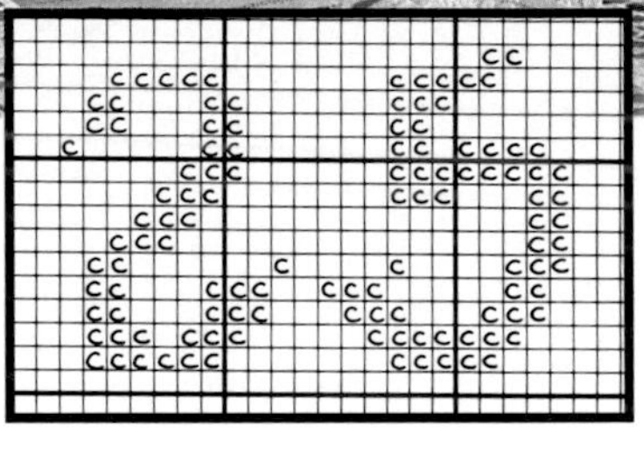

Wedding Anniversaries

SAMPLES

Samples in photograph were stitched on ice blue 28-count Annabelle over 2 threads for 25-year anniversary and on ivory 28-count Annabelle over 2 threads for 50-year anniversary. Design area is 5¾" x 5⅜" for each. Fabric was cut 12" x 12" for each.

To personalize design, transfer desired letters and numbers to graph paper, allowing 1 space between letters, 1 space between numbers, and 3 spaces between words. To determine center of names, count total number of spaces and divide by 2. Begin stitching center of names in center of area reserved for names in design. In same manner, center and stitch date below. If stitching 25-year anniversary, substitute "25" in design; center and stitch in space provided.

FABRICS	DESIGN AREAS
11-count	7¼" x 7⅛"
14-count	5¾" x 5⅝"
18-count	4½" x 4⅜"
22-count	3⅝" x 3½"

80

78

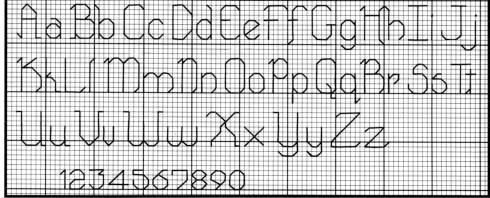

DMC Colors
(used for sample)
Step 1: Cross-stitch (2 strands)

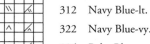

312   Navy Blue-lt.

322   Navy Blue-vy. lt.

334   Baby Blue-med.

503   Blue Green-med.

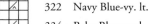

776   Pink-med.

899   Rose-med.

3325   Baby Blue-lt.

3326   Rose-lt.

002   Balger HL Gold (for 50 years)

001   Balger HL Silver (for 25 years)

Step 2: Backstitch (1 strand, except where noted)

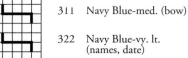

311   Navy Blue-med. (bow)

322   Navy Blue-vy. lt. (names, date)

502   Blue Green (stems)

899   Rose-med. (2 strands) ("years of wedded bliss")

CHAPTER 4
LOVE & CHERISH

"How do I love thee ...?"
— Elizabeth Barrett Browning

*"Count the ways" with each stitch of love. I designed
these projects for you to display your devotion for all to see.
Commemorate your wedding day—when two lives
entwine, two hearts become one. The special person in
your life is sure to feel the love and affection in every stitch.*

With love,

Alma Lynne

A Beary Special Couple

SAMPLES

Samples in photograph were stitched on periwinkle 28-count Pastel Linen over 2 threads for small mirror frame and on rose 18-count lacy pillow sham over 2 threads. Design areas are 3½" x 3½" for small mirror frame and 5½" x 5½" for lacy pillow sham. Fabric was cut 9½" x 9½" for small mirror frame.

For pillow, center design in fabric area and begin stitching. For mirror frame, follow manufacturer's instructions for assembly.

Small mirror frame (Stock No. R-3909) was supplied by Sudberry House, P.O. Box 895, Old Lyme, CT 06371.

Lacy pillow sham (Stock No. 6305) was supplied by Tish and Amy Originals, P.O. Box 514, Centreville, AL 35042.

FABRICS	DESIGN AREAS
11-count	4½" x 4½"
14-count	3½" x 3½"
18-count	2¾" x 2¾"
22-count	2¼" x 2¼"

MATERIALS (for pillow)

Completed cross-stitch on rose 18-count lacy pillow sham
3 yards (¼"-wide) cream satin ribbon; matching thread
3 yards (¼"-wide) pink satin ribbon
3 yards (¼"-wide) green satin ribbon
3 yards (¼"-wide) light blue satin ribbon
3 yards (¼"-wide) medium blue satin ribbon
12" pillow form

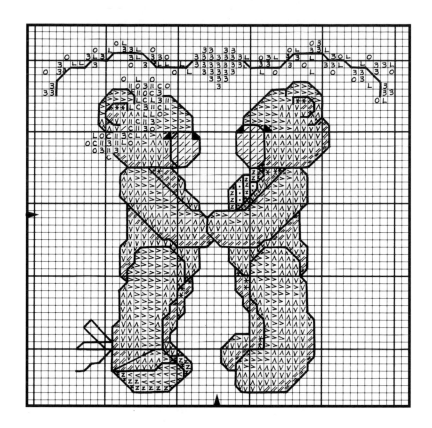

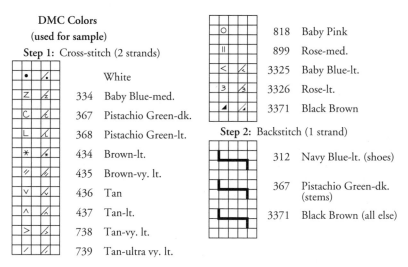

DMC Colors
(used for sample)

Step 1: Cross-stitch (2 strands)

•	╱			White
Z	╱		334	Baby Blue-med.
C	╱		367	Pistachio Green-dk.
L	╱		368	Pistachio Green-lt.
*	╱		434	Brown-lt.
″	╱		435	Brown-vy. lt.
V	╱		436	Tan
∧	╱		437	Tan-lt.
>	╱		738	Tan-vy. lt.
╱	╱		739	Tan-ultra vy. lt.

O	╱		818	Baby Pink
II	╱		899	Rose-med.
<	╱		3325	Baby Blue-lt.
3	╱		3326	Rose-lt.
◢	╱		3371	Black Brown

Step 2: Backstitch (1 strand)

	312	Navy Blue-lt. (shoes)
	367	Pistachio Green-dk. (stems)
	3371	Black Brown (all else)

INSTRUCTIONS

Cut each ribbon into 3 equal lengths. Separate ribbons into 3 sets, with each set containing 1 ribbon of each color. Handling all ribbons as 1, twist 1 set of ribbons to form an 11" coil in center of length. Tack each end of coil to top left and right corners of pillow, leaving tails. Handling all ribbons as 1, tie 1 set of ribbons into a bow and tack to top left corner. Repeat with remaining set of ribbons for top right corner (see photograph). Trim ends of ribbons at an angle.

Tulip Trio

SAMPLES

Samples in photograph were stitched on cream 28-count Pastel Linen over 2 threads for Tiny Tulip on pill box, Large Tulip on small silver box, and Tulip with Bow on crystal powder box. Design areas are ⅞" x ¾" for Tiny Tulip, 2⅞" x 2⅝" for Large Tulip, and 2⅜" x 2⅜" for Tulip with Bow. Fabric was cut 4" x 4" for Tiny Tulip and 7" x 7" each for Large Tulip and Tulip with Bow.

Pill box (Stock No. PB), small silver box (Stock No. ST3), and crystal powder box (Stock No. CT4) were supplied by Anne Brinkley Designs, 246 Walnut Street, Newton, MA 02160.

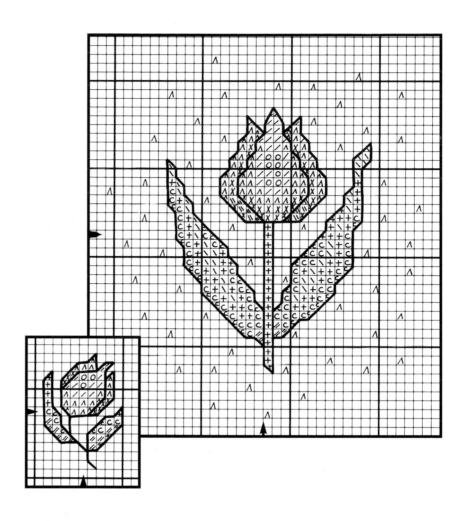

Tiny Tulip

FABRICS	DESIGN AREAS
11-count	1⅛" x ⅞"
14-count	⅞" x ¾"
18-count	¾" x ½"
22-count	⅝" x ½"

13
9

Large Tulip

FABRICS	DESIGN AREAS
11-count	3¾" x 3¼"
14-count	2⅞" x 2⅝"
18-count	2¼" x 2"
22-count	1⅞" x 1⅝"

41
36

Tiny Tulip

DMC Colors
(used for sample)

Step 1: Cross-stitch (2 strands)

″	⌀	319	Pistachio Green-vy. dk.
+	⊿	320	Pistachio Green-med.
C	∠	367	Pistachio Green-dk.
∕	∠	776	Pink-med.
O		818	Baby Pink
	∠	899	Rose-med.
∧	∠	3326	Rose-lt.

Step 2: Backstitch (1 strand)

	309	Rose-deep (flower)
	890	Pistachio Green-ultra dk. (stem)

Large Tulip

DMC Colors
(used for sample)

Step 1: Cross-stitch (2 strands)

″	⌀	319	Pistachio Green-vy. dk.
+	⊿	320	Pistachio Green-med.
∖∖	∧	335	Rose
C	∠	367	Pistachio Green-dk.
∖	∠	368	Pistachio Green-lt.
∕	∕	776	Pink-med.
O		818	Baby Pink
X		899	Rose-med.
∧	∠	3326	Rose-lt.

Step 2: Backstitch (1 strand)

	309	Rose-deep (flower)
	890	Pistachio Green-ultra dk. (leaves, stem)

Tulip with Bow

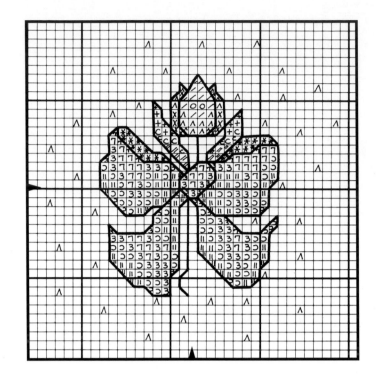

FABRICS

11-count		DESIGN AREAS
11-count		3⅛" x 3⅛"
14-count		2⅜" x 2⅜"
18-count		1⅞" x 1⅞"
22-count		1½" x 1½"

34 ↑ → 33

DMC Colors
(used for sample)

Step 1: Cross-stitch (2 strands)

✻ /	312	Navy Blue-lt.
∥	319	Pistachio Green-vy. dk.
+	320	Pistachio Green-med.
∥	322	Navy Blue-vy. lt.
⊃	334	Baby Blue-med.
C	367	Pistachio Green-dk.
7	775	Baby Blue-vy. lt.
/	776	Pink-med.
O	818	Baby Pink
X	899	Rose-med.
3	3325	Baby Blue-lt.
∧	3326	Rose-lt.

Step 2: Backstitch (1 strand)

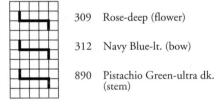

	309	Rose-deep (flower)
	312	Navy Blue-lt. (bow)
	890	Pistachio Green-ultra dk. (stem)

Alphabet for Rose Monogram

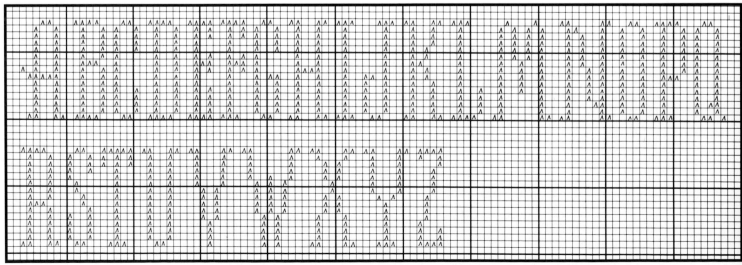

Rose
Monogram

SAMPLE

Sample in photograph was stitched on white 28-count Annabelle over 2 threads. Design area is 2¾" x 2¾". Fabric was cut 9" x 9".

Crystal container (Stock No. CT3) was supplied by Anne Brinkley Designs, 246 Walnut Street, Newton, MA 02160.

FABRICS	DESIGN AREAS
11-count	3½" x 3½"
14-count	2¾" x 2¾"
18-count	2⅛" x 2⅛"
22-count	1¾" x 1¾"

39
39

DMC Colors
(used for sample)

Step 1: Cross-stitch (2 strands)

*	⁄	309	Rose-deep
⁄	⁄	335	Rose
\\	⁄	500	Blue Green-vy. dk.
v	⁄	501	Blue Green-dk.
⊃	⁄	502	Blue Green
<	⁄	503	Blue Green-med.
I	⁄	504	Blue Green-lt.
C	⁄	776	Pink-med.
O	⁄	818	Baby Pink
⁄	⁄	819	Baby Pink-lt.
∧	⁄	899	Rose-med.
\	⁄	3326	Rose-lt.

Step 2: Backstitch (1 strand)

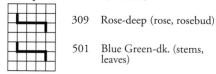

	309	Rose-deep (rose, rosebud)
	501	Blue Green-dk. (stems, leaves)

Wedding Angels

SAMPLES

Samples in photograph were stitched on cream 28-count Pastel Linen over 2 threads. Design areas are 6⅜" x 13⅜" for pillow and 11⅛" x 13⅜" for framed piece. Fabric was cut 13" x 20" for pillow and 18" x 20" for framed piece.

To personalize design, transfer desired letters from alphabet to graph paper, allowing 3 spaces between words and 1 space between numbers. To determine center for names, count total number of spaces in each word and divide each by 2. Begin stitching center of names in center of area reserved for names in design. In same manner, center and stitch date below name.

Note: Use alphabet from "Wedding Place Cards and Pillow," page 83, for personalization.

Pillow

FABRICS	DESIGN AREAS
11-count	8⅛" x 17⅛"
14-count	6⅜" x 13⅜"
18-count	5" x 10½"
22-count	4" x 8½"

89
→ 188

Framed Piece

FABRICS	DESIGN AREAS
11-count	14⅛" x 17⅛"
14-count	11⅛" x 13⅜"
18-count	8⅝" x 10½"
22-count	7" x 8½"

155
→ 188

MATERIALS (for pillow)

Completed cross-stitch on cream 28-count Pastel Linen; matching thread
¼ yard of unstitched cream 28-count Pastel Linen
1¼ yard (4"-wide) pregathered cream lace edging
1¼ yard (½"-wide) nylon binding
1¼ yard (¼"-wide) blue satin ribbon
Stuffing

INSTRUCTIONS

All seam allowances are ¼".

1. With design centered, trim Pastel Linen to 8" x 15¼". From unstitched Pastel Linen, cut 1 (8" x 15¼") piece for pillow back.

2. With right sides facing and raw edges aligned, stitch pillow front to back, leaving an opening for turning. Trim corners; turn and stuff. Slipstitch opening closed.

3. To make casing on lace, sew nylon binding ¼" from gathered edge of lace. Run satin ribbon through casing. Tack cut ends of ribbon to lace at each end.

4. To attach lace to pillow front, turn 1 cut end of lace under ½" and, beginning at center bottom, tack lace in place along bottom edge of pillow. When ends meet, turn remaining cut end under ½" and tack.

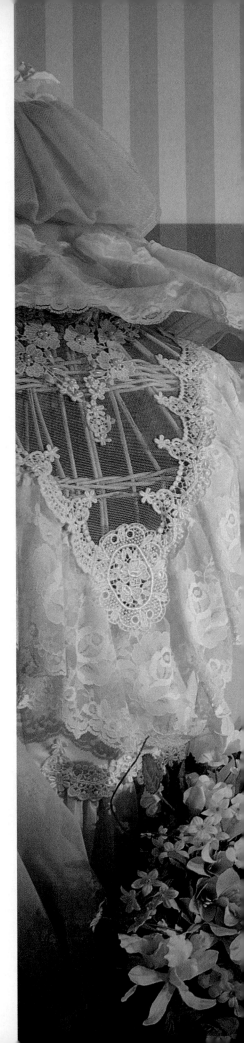

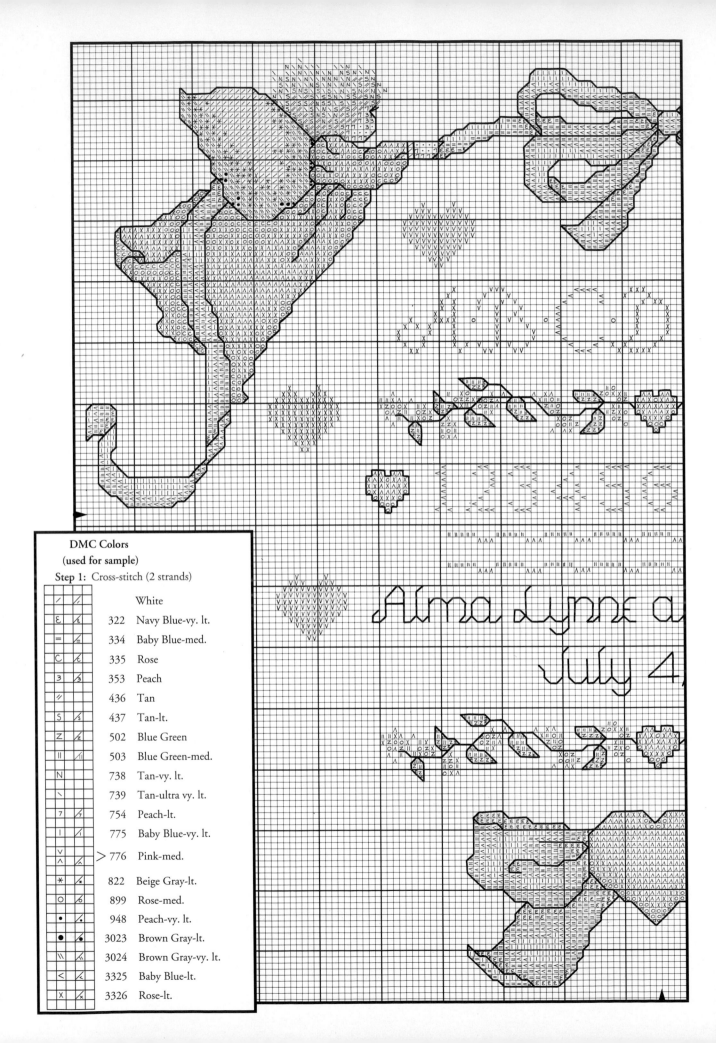

DMC Colors
(used for sample)

Step 1: Cross-stitch (2 strands)

/	/		White
Ɛ	ɛ	322	Navy Blue-vy. lt.
=	≤	334	Baby Blue-med.
C	ℓ	335	Rose
3	3	353	Peach
//		436	Tan
S	5	437	Tan-lt.
Z	z	502	Blue Green
||	//|	503	Blue Green-med.
N		738	Tan-vy. lt.
\		739	Tan-ultra vy. lt.
7	7	754	Peach-lt.
I	/	775	Baby Blue-vy. lt.
V / ∧	∧	⟩ 776	Pink-med.
*	/*	822	Beige Gray-lt.
O	6	899	Rose-med.
•	/.	948	Peach-vy. lt.
●	/●	3023	Brown Gray-lt.
\\	\\	3024	Brown Gray-vy. lt.
<	/<	3325	Baby Blue-lt.
X	/x	3326	Rose-lt.

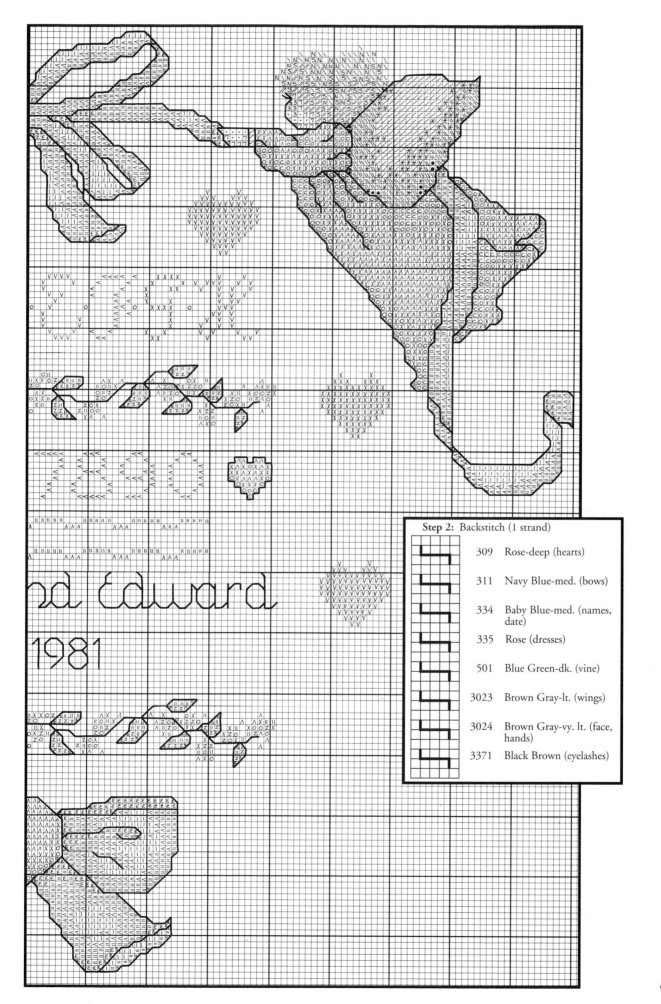

nd Edward

1981

Step 2: Backstitch (1 strand)

	309	Rose-deep (hearts)
	311	Navy Blue-med. (bows)
	334	Baby Blue-med. (names, date)
	335	Rose (dresses)
	501	Blue Green-dk. (vine)
	3023	Brown Gray-lt. (wings)
	3024	Brown Gray-vy. lt. (face, hands)
	3371	Black Brown (eyelashes)

Wedding Place Cards and Pillow

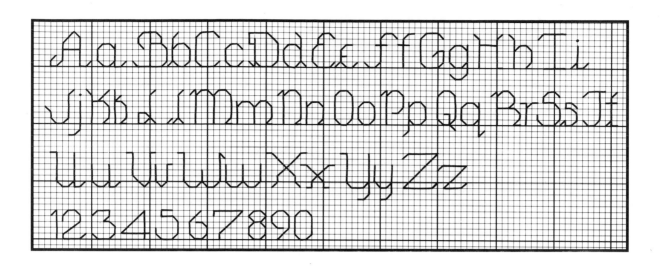

SAMPLES

Samples in photograph were stitched on white 14-count perforated paper over 1 thread and on white 10-count Victorian Lacy Pillow over 1 thread. Design areas are 1⅜" x 3½" for each place card and 3⅝" x 3¾" for pillow. Paper was cut 4" x 4" for each place card. Fold paper in half widthwise.

To personalize place card design, transfer desired letters from alphabet to graph paper. To determine center of name, count total number of spaces and divide by 2. Center and stitch design and name on 1 side of folded paper. Embellish with bow in top left corner.

Victorian Lacy Pillow (Stock No. V-6601) was supplied by Tish and Amy Originals, P.O. Box 514, Centreville, AL 35042.

Pillow

FABRICS	DESIGN AREAS
11-count	3¼" x 3⅜"
14-count	2⅝" x 2⅝"
18-count	2" x 2"
22-count	1⅝" x 1⅝"

36
↑
↳ 37

MATERIALS (for pillow)

Completed cross-stitch on Victorian Lacy Pillow
1 yard (⅝"-wide) green satin ribbon; matching thread
1½ yards (⅝"-wide) pink satin ribbon; matching thread
1 package beaded bridal sprays

INSTRUCTIONS

Cut green and pink satin ribbons into 4 equal lengths each. Referring to photograph, fold 1 green satin ribbon to form a loop and tack to 1 corner of pillow. Repeat with remaining green satin ribbons and pillow corners. Tie each pink satin ribbon into a bow and tack 1 to each green satin ribbon loop. Embellish each corner with 1 bridal spray, inserting end through lace just below bow. To hide raw end of bridal spray, insert into pillow back.

Place Card

FABRICS	DESIGN AREAS
11-count	1⅞" x 4½"
14-count	1⅜" x 3½"
18-count	1⅛" x 2¾"
22-count	⅞" x 2¼"

20
↑
↳ 49

DMC Colors
(used for sample)

Step 1: Cross-stitch (2 strands)

v		503	Blue Green-med.
C		3326	Rose-lt.

Step 2: Backstitch (2 strands)

		503	Blue Green-med.

DMC Colors
(used for sample)

Step 1: Cross-stitch (2 strands)

x	⩘	502	Blue Green
z	⩘	503	Blue Green-med.
O	⩘	504	Blue Green-lt.
v	⩘	776	Pink-med.
\		818	Baby Pink
⁄⁄		899	Rose-med.
C		3326	Rose-lt.

Step 2: Backstitch (1 strand)

	502	Blue Green (leaves, vines)
	899	Rose-med. (hearts)

Bows and Lace

SAMPLE

Sample in photograph was stitched on white 18-count hand towel over 2 threads. Design area is 1¼" x 12½". Center design in fabric area and begin stitching.

Lace hand towel (Stock No. 2001) was supplied by Tish and Amy Originals, P.O. Box 514, Centreville, AL 35042.

FABRICS	DESIGN AREAS
11-count	1" x 10¾"
14-count	¾" x 8⅜"
18-count	⅝" x 6½"
22-count	½" x 5⅜"

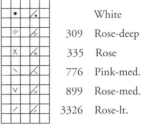

Step 1: Cross-stitch (2 strands)

•	∕•		White
⁄⁄	⁄⁄	309	Rose-deep
X	⁄x	335	Rose
\	\	776	Pink-med.
v	⁄v	899	Rose-med.
∕	⁄∕	3326	Rose-lt.

Step 2: Backstitch (1 strand)

		326	Rose-vy. dk.

11

118

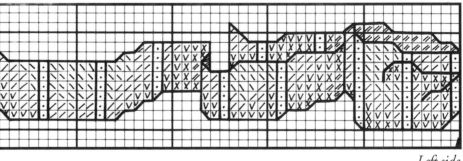

Left side

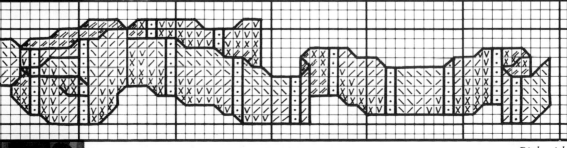

Right side

Dresser Set

SAMPLES

Samples in photograph were stitched on white 14-count Astoria over 1 thread for dresser runner and on white 28-count Bridal Alma Cloth over 1 thread for mirror and brush. Design areas are 8½" x 6" for dresser runner and 4⅛" x 4⅞" each for mirror and brush. Fabric was cut 64" x 25" for dresser runner and 11" x 11" each for mirror and brush.

For dresser runner, center and stitch design on each short edge, leaving 3½" of unworked fabric below design. For mirror and brush, follow manufacturer's instructions for assembly.

Dresser set (Stock No. SSET) was supplied by Anne Brinkley Designs, 246 Walnut Street, Newton, MA 02160.

FABRICS	DESIGN AREAS
11-count	10⅞" x 7¼"
14-count	8½" x 5¾"
18-count	6⅝" x 4½"
22-count	5⅜" x 3⅝"

119

→ 80

MATERIALS (for runner)

Completed cross-stitch on white
  14-count Astoria; matching
  thread
4⅔ yards (¼"-wide) nylon binding
4⅔ yards (2½"-wide) off-white
  pregathered lace edging

INSTRUCTIONS

1. Trim fabric to 57½" x 18½". With right sides facing and raw
edges aligned, fold fabric in half lengthwise. Cut ends to form scalloped edges. Unfold.

2. Turn all edges under ¼" and stitch around entire runner.

3. Using ¼" nylon binding, stitch lace edging to wrong side of
runner.

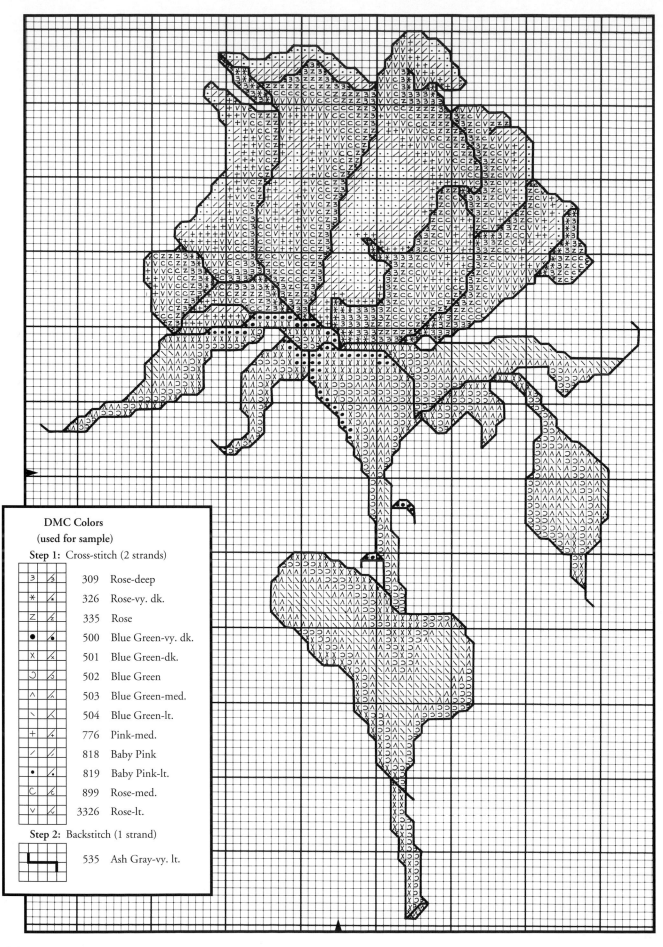

DMC Colors

(used for sample)

Step 1: Cross-stitch (2 strands)

3	3	309	Rose-deep
*	*	326	Rose-vy. dk.
Z	Z	335	Rose
●	●	500	Blue Green-vy. dk.
X	X	501	Blue Green-dk.
◡	◡	502	Blue Green
∧	∧	503	Blue Green-med.
\	\	504	Blue Green-lt.
+	+	776	Pink-med.
/	/	818	Baby Pink
•	•	819	Baby Pink-lt.
C	C	899	Rose-med.
V	V	3326	Rose-lt.

Step 2: Backstitch (1 strand)

		535	Ash Gray-vy. lt.

Ivy Pillowcases

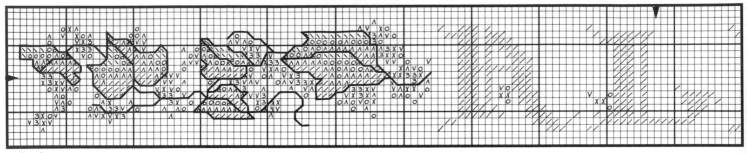

Left side

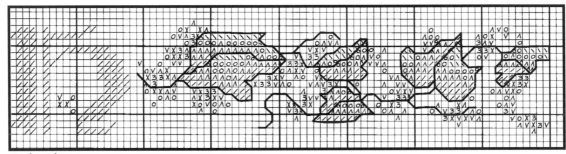

Right side

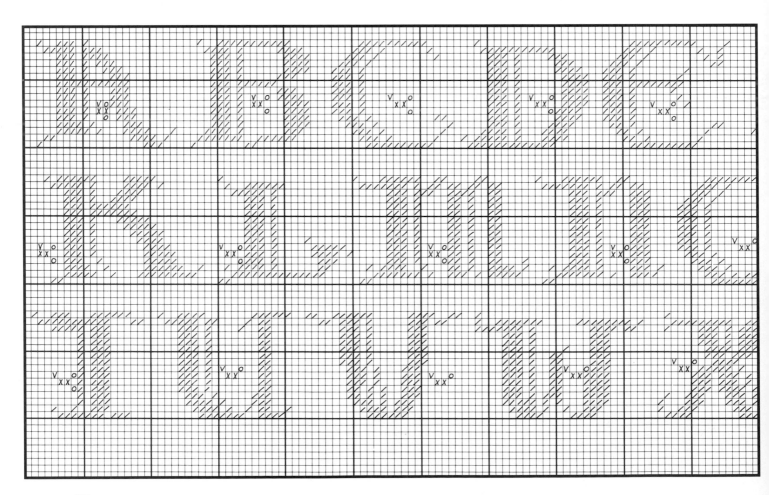

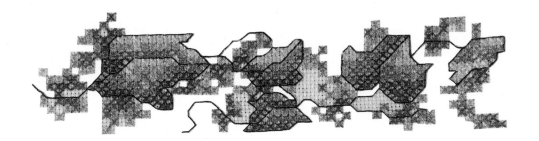

SAMPLES

Samples in photograph were stitched on white 18-count Victorian pillow-cases over 2 threads. Design area is 1¾" x 20¾" for each. Center design in Aida area and begin stitching.

To personalize design, transfer desired letters to graph paper, allow-ing 1 space between each letter. To determine center of initials, count total number of spaces and divide by 2. Begin stitching center of initials in center of area reserved for initials in design.

Victorian pillowcases (Stock No. V-2501) were supplied by Tish and Amy Originals, P.O. Box 514, Centreville, AL 35042.

FABRICS	DESIGN AREAS
11-count	1½" x 17"
14-count	1⅛" x 13⅜"
18-count	⅞" x 10⅜"
22-count	¾" x 8½"

16 ↑
→ 187

DMC Colors
(used for sample)

Step 1: Cross-stitch (2 strands)

X	⟋	223	Shell Pink-med.
V	⟋	224	Shell Pink-lt.
⟋	⟋	501	Blue Green-dk.
^	⟋	502	Blue Green
O	⟋	503	Blue Green-med.
⟍	⟋	504	Blue Green-lt.
3	⟋	3722	Shell Pink

Step 2: Backstitch (1 strand)

⌐_	500 Blue Green-vy. dk.

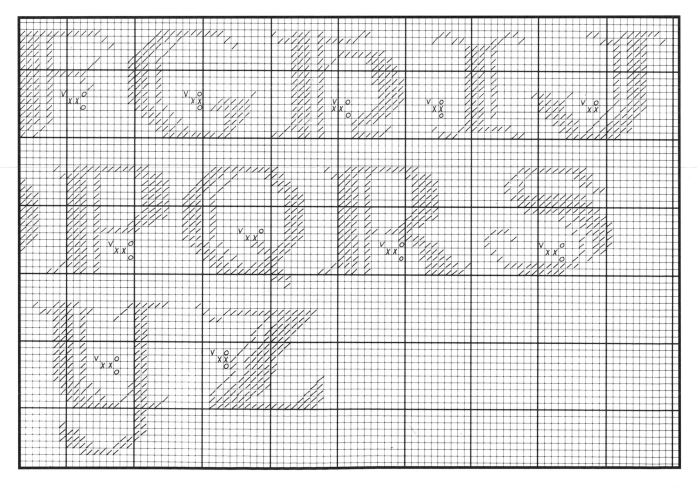

CHAPTER 5
BABY'S KEEPSAKES

*"It is not a slight thing when they,
who are so fresh from God, love us."*
— *Charles Dickens*

What greater gifts could be given a woman than children—tiny extensions of ourselves looking to us for life. Children everywhere, and especially my precious Clay and Seth, bring such joy and happiness. My motherhood sings of the wonder of them.

I hope the designs in this chapter will one day become keepsakes for your children, who will feel the love and care that went into each stitch of your needle.

With joy and happiness,

Alma Lynne

Rose Garland Baby Blanket

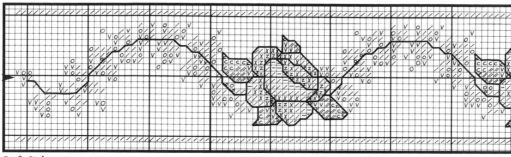

Left Side

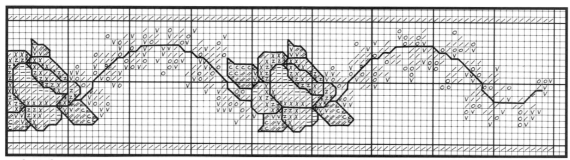

Right Side

SAMPLE

Sample in photograph was stitched on white 19-count Baby's Blanket over 2 threads. Design area is 2⅜" x 18⅛".

Center and stitch design on each short end and each long side of afghan, leaving corner squares and center area unstitched (see photograph).

Baby's Blanket (Stock No. 990-6180) was supplied by Janlynn Corporation, 34 Front Street, Indian Orchard, MA 01151.

Note: Graph shows border on top and bottom of garland motif that was not stitched on afghan.

FABRICS	DESIGN AREAS
11-count	2" x 15⅝"
14-count	1⅝" x 12¼"
18-count	1¼" x 9½"
22-count	1" x 7⅞"

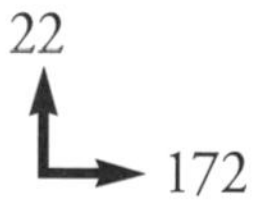

22 ↑ → 172

MATERIALS

Completed cross-stitch on white 19-count Baby's Blanket
11¼ yards (⅛"-wide) pink satin ribbon

INSTRUCTIONS

Cut ribbon into 4 (25") lengths, 4 (30") lengths, and 4 (45") lengths. Referring to photograph and staggering placement, thread 2 (30") lengths through openings in decorative weave along 1 short end of afghan, leaving tails at start and finish. Repeat with remaining 30" lengths on remaining short end. Thread 2 (45") lengths through openings in decorative weave along 1 long side of afghan, leaving tails at start and finish. Repeat with remaining 45" lengths on remaining long side. Where decorative weave intersects at each corner, tie ribbon tails into a knot. Tie 1 (25") length of ribbon into a bow with several 2" loops. Tie to 1 corner with woven ribbon tails. Repeat with remaining ribbons and corners (see photograph).

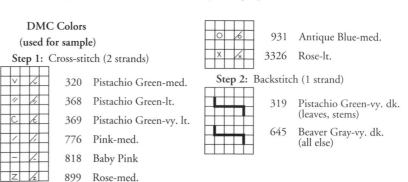

DMC Colors
(used for sample)
Step 1: Cross-stitch (2 strands)

V		320	Pistachio Green-med.
/		368	Pistachio Green-lt.
C		369	Pistachio Green-vy. lt.
/		776	Pink-med.
–		818	Baby Pink
Z		899	Rose-med.

O	6	931	Antique Blue-med.
X	⟋	3326	Rose-lt.

Step 2: Backstitch (1 strand)

		319	Pistachio Green-vy. dk. (leaves, stems)
		645	Beaver Gray-vy. dk. (all else)

Our Baby's Keepsakes

SAMPLE

Sample in photograph was stitched on off-white 27-count linen bag over 2 threads. Design area is 5" x 6". Center design on bag front and begin stitching.

Linen bag (Stock No. 977315) was supplied by Janlynn Corporation, 34 Front Street, Indian Orchard, MA 01151.

FABRICS	DESIGN AREAS
11-count	5¾" x 6⅝"
14-count	4⅝" x 5¼"
18-count	3½" x 4"
22-count	2⅞" x 3⅜"

63
↑
└→ 74

MATERIALS

⅝ yard (2¼"-wide) off-white pregathered lace edging; matching thread

1½ yards (¼"-wide) light blue grosgrain ribbon; matching thread

1½ yards (⅜"-wide) medium blue grosgrain ribbon

1 yard (⅝"-wide) medium blue grosgrain ribbon

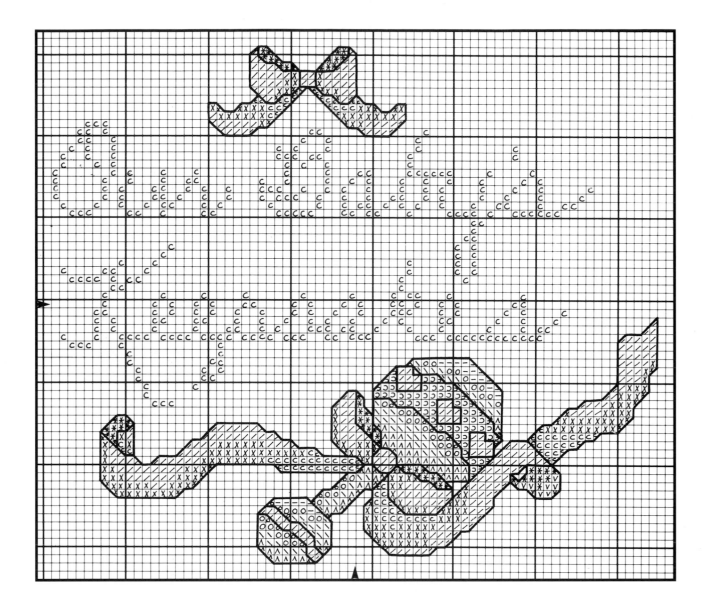

DMC Colors
(used for sample)

Step 1: Cross-stitch (2 strands)

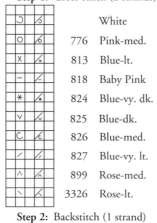

⊃	⁄		White
O	⁄	776	Pink-med.
X	⁄	813	Blue-lt.
–	⁄	818	Baby Pink
*	⁄	824	Blue-vy. dk.
v	⁄	825	Blue-dk.
C	⁄	826	Blue-med.
⁄	⁄	827	Blue-vy. lt.
∧	⁄	899	Rose-med.
＼	⁄	3326	Rose-lt.

Step 2: Backstitch (1 strand)

⌐	3371 Black Brown

INSTRUCTIONS

1. For lace edging, with right sides facing and beginning at back of bag, align bound edge of lace with top edge of bag. Stitch lace in place around top of bag. When ends of lace meet, fold unstitched end under; overlap and stitch.

2. For tote handles, cut ⅝"-wide medium blue ribbon in half. Fold each end of 1 ribbon under 1". Place folded ends inside front top edge of tote, 2" from each side, and stitch in place. Repeat with remaining half of ribbon, stitching ends to inside back of tote.

3. Cut ¼"-wide light blue and ⅜"-wide medium blue ribbon in half. Handling 1 length of each as a single unit, tie into a bow. Repeat with remaining lengths. Referring to photograph, tack bows to top left and right corners. Trim ends of ribbons at an angle.

Everything's Ducky

SAMPLES

Samples in photograph were stitched on white 14-count Celebration Pillow over 2 threads, on white 11-count Celebration Coverlet over 2 threads, on white 14-count Celebration Toddler Bib over 2 threads, and on white 14-count Celebration Hamper Bag over 2 threads. Design areas are 5¼" x 5¼" for pillow, 7¼" x 7¼" for coverlet, 2⅞" x 7⅝" for bib, and 2¼" x 14¾" for hamper bag. Embellish pillow, coverlet, and hamper bag with various colored ribbons, if desired (see photograph).

Celebration Pillow (Stock No. 977-318), Celebration Coverlet (Stock No. 990-6168), Celebration Toddler Bib (Stock No. 990-6164), and Celebration Hamper Bag (Stock No. 990-6166) were supplied by Janlynn Corporation, 34 Front Street, Indian Orchard, MA 01151.

Note: When stitching pillow, use inside border of Ducky with Double Border graph; when stitching coverlet, center ducky from Ducky with Hearts in a double border.

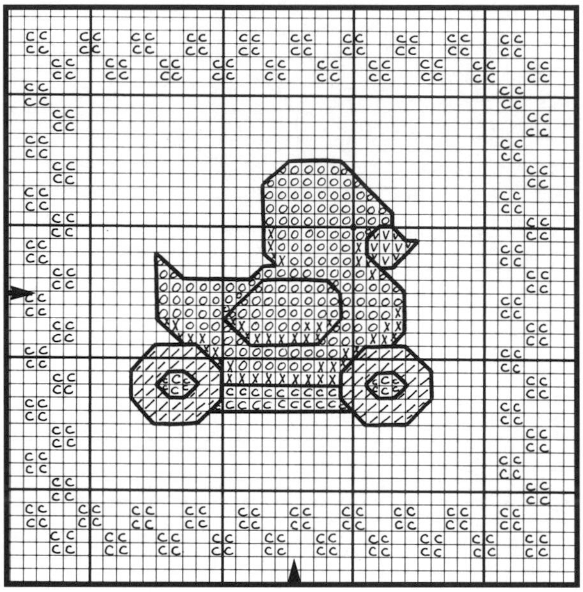

Ducky with Double Border

Ducky Single Border (Pillow)

FABRICS	DESIGN SIZES
11-count	3¼" x 3¼"
14-count	2⅝" x 2⅝"
18-count	2" x 2"
22-count	1⅝" x 1⅝"

36 x 36

Ducky Double Border (Coverlet)

FABRICS	DESIGN AREAS
11-count	3⅝" x 3⅝"
14-count	2⅞" x 2⅞"
18-count	2¼" x 2¼"
22-count	1⅞" x 1⅞"

40 x 40

DMC Colors
(used for sample)

Step 1: Cross-stitch (2 strands)

Symbol	DMC	Color
X	744	Yellow-pale
O	745	Yellow-lt. pale
C	809 / 3326	Delft (for boy) / Rose-lt. (for girl)
/	3326	Rose-lt.
V	3341	Apricot

Step 2: Backstitch (1 strand)

3371 Black Brown

Step 3: French Knot (1 strand)

3371 Black Brown (eye)

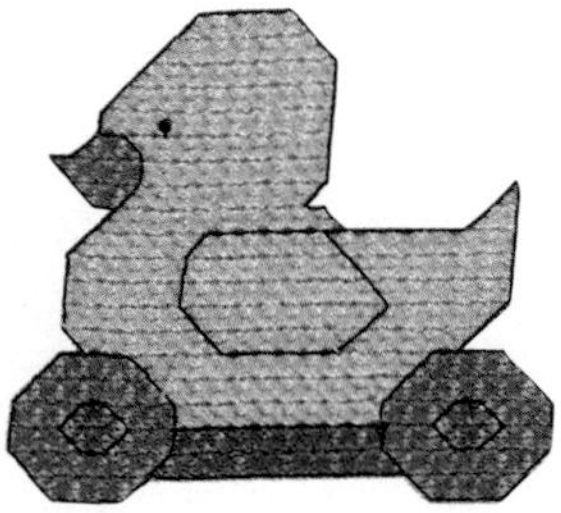

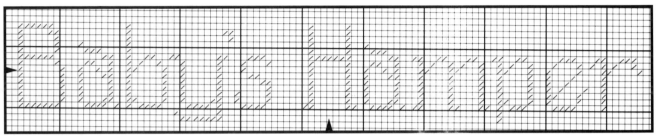

Ducky with Hearts

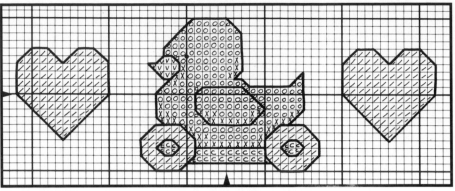

Hamper Bag

Ducky with Hearts (Bib)

FABRICS	DESIGN AREAS
11-count	1⅞" x 4⅞"
14-count	1⅜" x 3⅞"
18-count	1⅛" x 3"
22-count	⅞" x 2½"

20
↑
└→ 54

Hamper Bag

FABRICS	DESIGN AREAS
11-count	1½" x 9⅜"
14-count	1⅛" x 7⅜"
18-count	⅞" x 5¾"
22-count	¾" x 4⅝"

16
↑
└→ 103

Ducky with Hearts (Bib)

DMC Colors
(used for sample)

Step 1: Cross-stitch (2 strands)

X	⟋	744	Yellow-pale
O	⟋	745	Yellow-lt. pale
C	⟋	809	Delft (for boy)
		3326	Rose-lt. (for girl)
⟋	⟋	3326	Rose-lt.
V	⟋	3341	Apricot

Step 2: Backstitch (1 strand)

3371   Black Brown

Step 3: French Knot (1 strand)

●   3371   Black Brown (eye)

Hamper Bag

DMC Colors
(used for sample)

Step 1: Cross-stitch (2 strands)

⟋   809   Delft

Birth Samplers

SAMPLES

Samples in photograph were stitched on white 18-count Tabby Cloth over 2 threads. Design area is 17" x 12⅝" for each. Fabric was cut 23" x 19" for each.

To stitch boy sampler, first complete upper section of sampler and all borders that divide sampler into 3 stitching areas. Arrows for centering boy design in middle section are provided on chart for girl. Match these arrows with those on boy chart and begin stitching boy and kites.

To personalize design, transfer desired letters and numbers from alphabet to graph paper, allowing 1 space between letters, 1 space between numbers, and 3 spaces between words. To determine center of name, count total number of spaces and divide by 2. Begin stitching center of name in center of area reserved for name in design. In same manner, center and stitch date below.

FABRICS | DESIGN AREAS

FABRICS	DESIGN AREAS
11-count	13⅞" x 10⅜"
14-count	10⅞" x 8⅛"
18-count	8½" x 6⅜"
22-count	7" x 5⅛"

153
→ 114

DMC Colors
(used for sample)

Step 1: Cross-stitch (2 strands)

•			White
9		309	Rose-deep
 3	>	335	Rose
/		501	Blue Green-dk.
Ø		503	Blue Green-med.
//		758	Terra Cotta-lt.
−		761	Salmon-lt.
L		762	Pearl Gray-vy. lt.
6		776	Pink-med.
*		797	Royal Blue
Ɛ		798	Delft-dk.
X		799	Delft-med.
I		800	Delft-pale
\		809	Delft
C		899	Rose-med.
V		950	Peach Pecan-dk.
Z		3326	Rose-lt.
ᴐ		3779	Terra Cotta-vy. lt.

Step 2: Backstitch (1 strand, except where noted)

	309 Rose-deep (bow)
	799 Delft-med. (2 strands) (name, date)
	820 Royal Blue-vy. dk. (hat)
	3031 Mocha Brown-vy. dk. (face, eyelash, collar, kites)

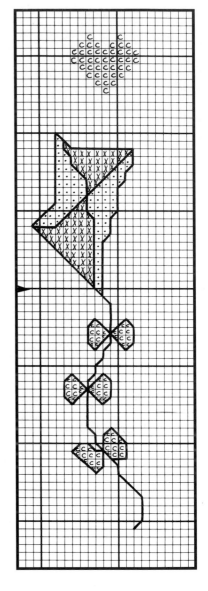

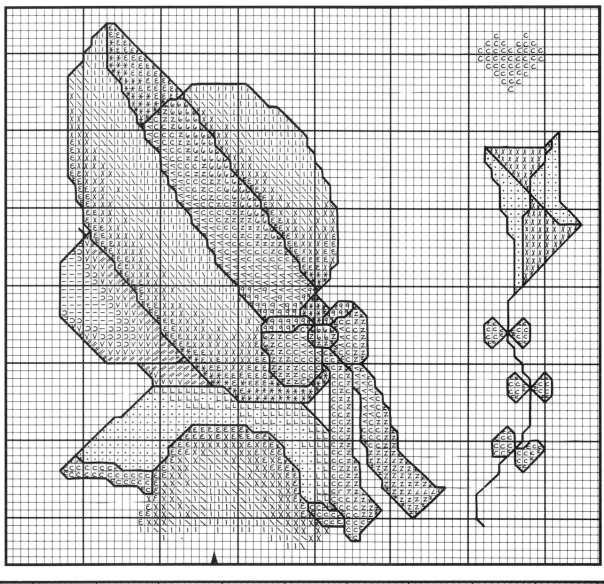

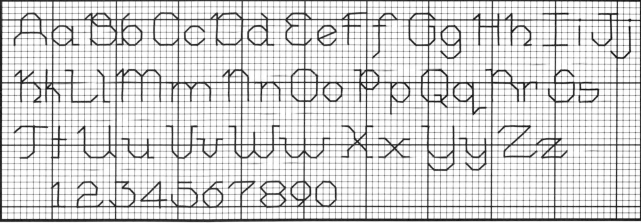

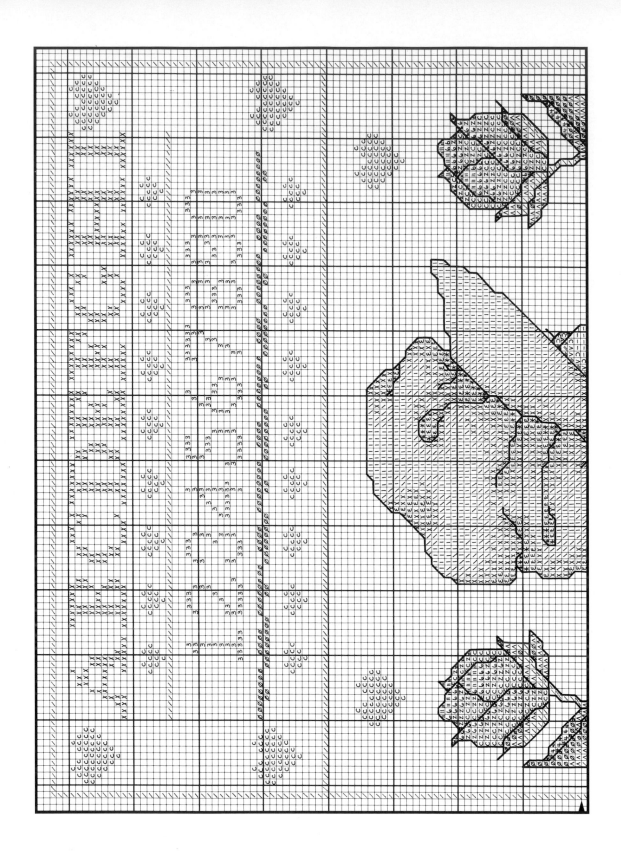

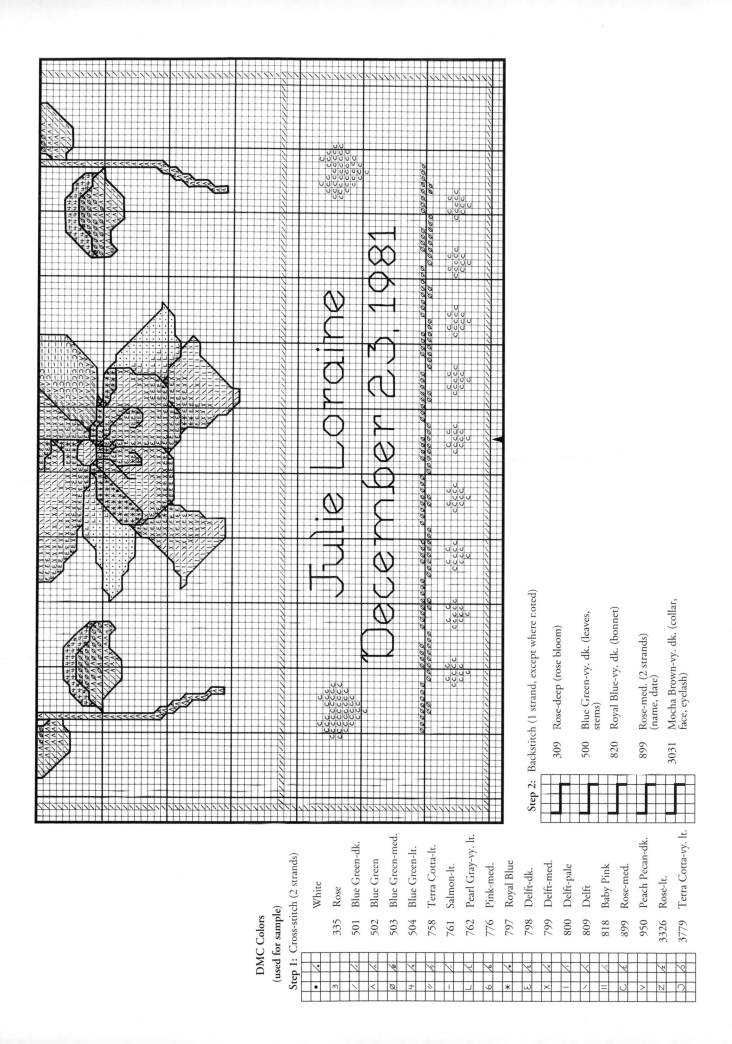

Julie Loraine

December 23, 1981

DMC Colors
(used for sample)

Step 1: Cross-stitch (2 strands)

•	White
3	335 Rose
/	501 Blue Green-dk.
∧	502 Blue Green
⊘	503 Blue Green-med.
+	504 Blue Green-lt.
∿	758 Terra Cotta-lt.
–	761 Salmon-lt.
L	762 Pearl Gray-vy. lt.
6	776 Pink-med.
*	797 Royal Blue
ε	798 Delft-dk.
X	799 Delft-med.
⌐	800 Delft-pale
∖	809 Delft
=	818 Baby Pink
C	899 Rose-med.
∨	950 Peach Pecan-dk.
Z	3326 Rose-lt.
⊃	3779 Terra Cotta-vy. lt.

Step 2: Backstitch (1 strand, except where noted)

309	Rose-deep (rose bloom)
500	Blue Green-vy. dk. (leaves, stems)
820	Royal Blue-vy. dk. (bonnet)
899	Rose-med. (2 strands) (name, date)
3031	Mocha Brown-vy. dk. (collar, face, eyelash)

Bunnies & Bears Bibs

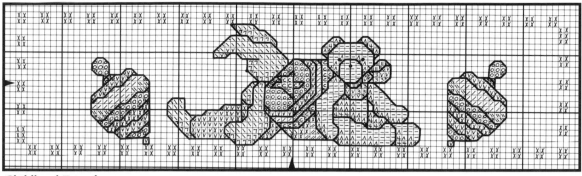

Childhood Friends

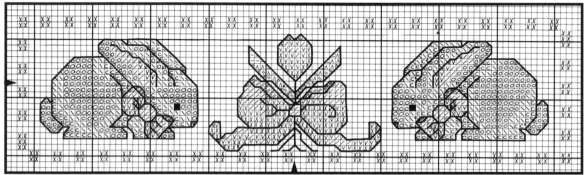

Bunnies with Bows

SAMPLES

Samples in photograph were stitched on blue 11-count bib over 1 thread and on pink 11-count bib over 1 thread. Design area is 2¼" x 8¾" for each. Center design in fabric area and begin stitching.

Baby bibs (Stock No. 11490 for blue bib, Stock No. 11492 for cream bib) were supplied by Leisure Arts, P.O. Box 5595, Little Rock, AR 72215.

Note: The pink bib used for 1 of the models has since been discontinued. We have supplied the stock number for the cream bib in its place.

FABRICS	DESIGN AREAS
11-count	2¼" x 8¾"
14-count	1¾" x 6⅞"
18-count	1⅜" x 5⅜"
22-count	1⅛" x 4⅜"

25
↑
└→ 96

Childhood Friends

DMC Colors
(used for sample)

Step 1: Cross-stitch (2 strands)

C	ℓ		White
⌃	⌃	676	Old Gold-lt.
−	⁄	677	Old Gold-vy. lt.
4	4	729	Old Gold-med.
\\	⫽	743	Yellow-med.
⁄	⁄	744	Yellow-pale
V	⩘	776	Pink-med.
⫽	⩘	792	Cornflower Blue-dk.
X 7	⩘ 7	> 793	Cornflower Blue-med.
\\	⩘	794	Cornflower Blue-lt.
‖	⫽	899	Rose-med.
O	⁄	955	Nile Green-lt.
3	⩘	3326	Rose-lt.

Step 2: Backstitch (1 strand)

680	Old Gold-dk. (bear)
792	Cornflower Blue-dk. (ball, bunny, tops)
899	Rose-med. (bow on bear, bunny's pants)

Step 3: French Knot (1 strand)

●	3371 Black Brown (noses, eyes)

Bunnies with Bows

DMC Colors
(used for sample)

Step 1: Cross-stitch (2 strands)

O	⁄		White
C	ℓ	415	Pearl Gray
\\	⩘	562	Jade-med.
⌃	⩘	563	Jade-lt.
−	⁄	564	Jade-vy. lt.
＼	⩘	762	Pearl Gray-vy. lt.
V	⩘	776	Pink-med.
⁄	⁄	818	Baby Pink
⫽	⩘	899	Rose-med.
X	⩘	3326	Rose-lt.
■		3371	Black Brown

Step 2: Backstitch (1 strand)

309	Rose-deep (bows, flowers)
414	Steel Gray-dk. (bunnies)
561	Jade-vy. dk. (stems, leaves)

Bunny Wabbit

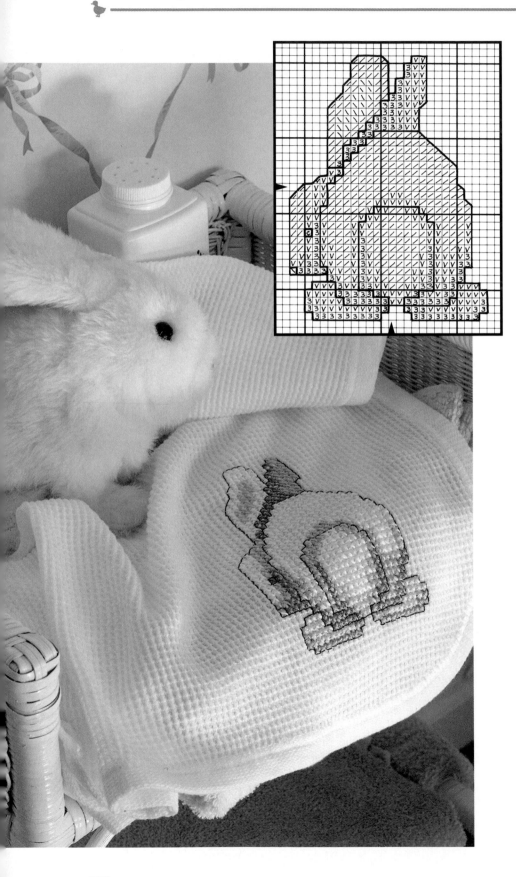

SAMPLE

Sample in photograph was stitched on white 6-count thermal receiving blanket over 1 thread. Design area is 6" x 4". Begin stitching in lower right corner, 1½" from bottom edge and 1¾" from right edge.

Thermal receiving blanket (Stock No. TIBR) was supplied by Designing Women Unlimited, 601 East 8th Street, El Dorado, AR 71730.

FABRICS	DESIGN AREAS
11-count	3⅛" x 2⅜"
14-count	2½" x 1⅞"
18-count	2" x 1½"
22-count	1⅝" x 1⅛"

35
26

DMC Colors
(used for sample)

Step 1: Cross-stitch (2 strands)

/	/		White
3		318	Steel Gray-lt.
V	/	762	Pearl Gray-vy. lt.
\		818	Baby Pink
C		899	Rose-med.

Step 2: Backstitch (1 strand)

		535	Ash Gray-vy. lt.

Hearts & Flowers Wash Mitt

SAMPLE

Sample in photograph was stitched on white 14-count wash mitt over 1 thread. Design area is 1½" x 4¾". Center design in fabric area and begin stitching.

Wash mitt (Stock No. 990-6111) was supplied by Janlynn Corporation, 34 Front Street, Indian Orchard, MA 01151.

FABRICS	DESIGN AREAS
11-count	1⅞" x 5¾"
14-count	1⅜" x 4⅝"
18-count	1⅛" x 3½"
22-count	⅞" x 2⅞"

20
64

MATERIALS

Completed cross-stitch on white 14-count wash mitt
Scrap of (¼"-wide) green satin ribbon; matching thread

INSTRUCTIONS

Referring to photograph, tie ribbon in a bow and tack in place.

DMC Colors
(used for sample)

Step 1: Cross-stitch (2 strands)

<	502 Blue Green
⌀	503 Blue Green-med.
3	899 Rose-med.
C	3325 Baby Blue-lt.
/	3326 Rose-lt.

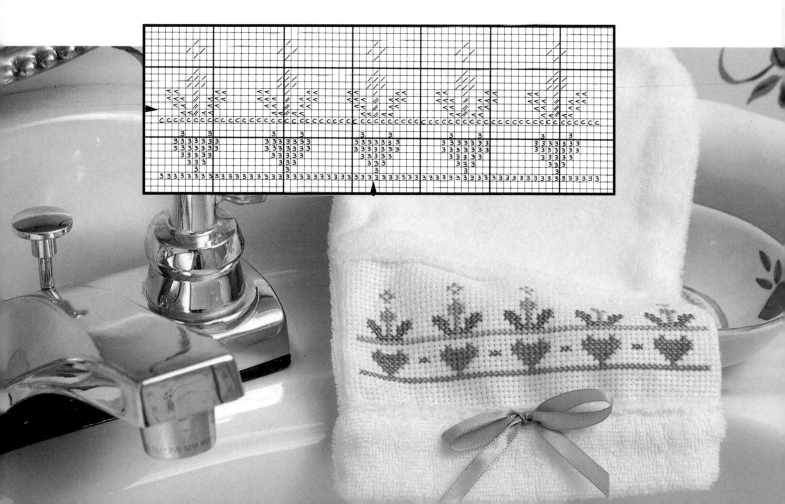

Baby Pillow

SAMPLE

Sample in photograph was stitched on blue 18-count pillow over 2 threads. Design area is 5¾" x 5⅛".

To personalize design, transfer desired letters and numbers from alphabet to graph paper, allowing 1 space between letters, 1 space between numbers, and 2 spaces between words. To determine center of name, count total number of spaces and divide by 2. Begin stitching center of name in center of area reserved for name in design. In same manner, center and stitch date below. Embellish pillow with ribbons as desired.

Pillow (Stock No. 6303) was supplied by Tish and Amy Originals, P.O. Box 514, Centreville, AL 35042.

FABRICS	DESIGN AREAS
11-count	4¾" x 4⅛"
14-count	3¾" x 3¼"
18-count	2⅞" x 2½"
22-count	2⅜" x 2⅛"

52
↑
└→ 46

DMC Colors
(used for sample)
Step 1: Cross-stitch (2 strands)

\	⟋		White
⟋	⟋	415	Pearl Gray
∧	⟋	502	Blue Green
⟋	⟋	504	Blue Green-lt.
7	7	762	Pearl Gray-vy. lt.
O	6	776	Pink-med.
V	⟋	809	Delft
X	⟋	899	Rose-med.

Step 2: Backstitch (1 strand)

502	Blue Green (stems)
799	Delft-med. (name, date)
3371	Black Brown (bow, heart)

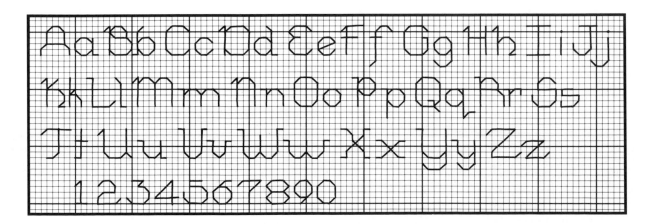

110

CHAPTER 6
HOLIDAY TREASURES
❖ ❖ ❖

"I never knew a holiday that deserved anything less than the grandest celebration."
— A. L. Hayden

Each holiday is special to me. I've even been accused of creating occasions to celebrate. Well, maybe that's true. We must live, love, and celebrate life, especially those times that deserve extra special attention. And believe me, I try!

Decorate your home for each and every holiday. And if one of those special celebrated days is your favorite, then add a little more! You can never, ever do too much!

Happy holidays,
Alma Lynne

Miniature Holiday Tree Skirts

SAMPLES

Samples in photograph were stitched over 2 threads on periwinkle 28-count Pastel Linen for Little Patriot Tree Skirt, on ivory 20-count Valerie for Little Witchie Tree Skirt, on white 25-count Lugana for Santa Tree Skirt, and on carnation 28-count Pastel Linen for Bunny Tree Skirt. Design areas are 5¾" x 2¾" for patriot, 3½" x 2½" for witch, 4½" x 2½" for Santa, and 2¼" x 3½" for bunny. Fabric was cut 17¼" x 17¼" for patriot tree skirt and 15½" x 15½" for all others.

Fold fabric square in half from top to bottom and again from left to right. Unfold fabric and, using dress-maker's pen, mark along creases to form cross. Along each marked line, center and begin stitching motif ¼" from bottom edge for patriot and Santa, and 1¾" from bottom for witch and bunny. Repeat along 3 marked lines, leaving 1 unstitched.

Little Patriot Motif

FABRICS	DESIGN AREAS
11-count	7" x 3¾"
14-count	5½" x 2⅞"
18-count	4¼" x 2¼"
22-count	3½" x 1⅞"

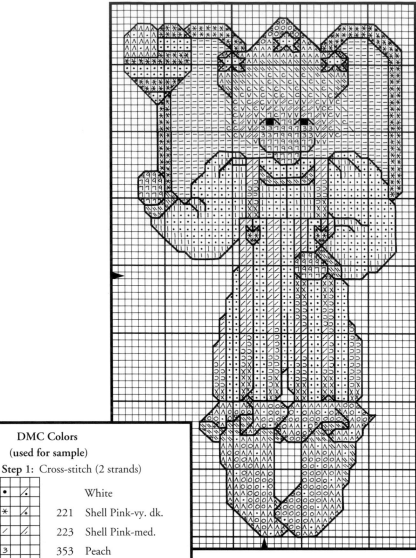

DMC Colors
(used for sample)

Step 1: Cross-stitch (2 strands)

•	⁄			White
*	⁄	221		Shell Pink-vy. dk.
⁄	⁄	223		Shell Pink-med.
3		353		Peach
⁄		435		Brown-vy. lt.
V		436		Tan
C		437		Tan-lt.
＼	⁄	738		Tan-vy. lt.
7	⁄	754		Peach-lt.
■		798		Delft-dk.
∧	⁄	930		Antique Blue-dk.
O	⁄	931		Antique Blue-med.
I	⁄	932		Antique Blue-lt.
9	⁄	948		Peach-vy. lt.
X	⁄	3721		Shell Pink-dk.
C	⁄	3722		Shell Pink
＼＼	⁄	3750		Antique Blue-vy. dk.
−	⁄	032		Balger Pearl Blending Filament

Step 2: Backstitch (1 strand)

L		3371	Black Brown

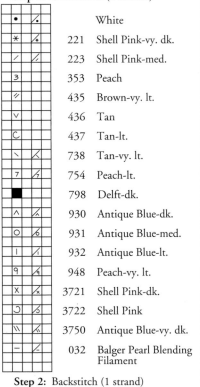

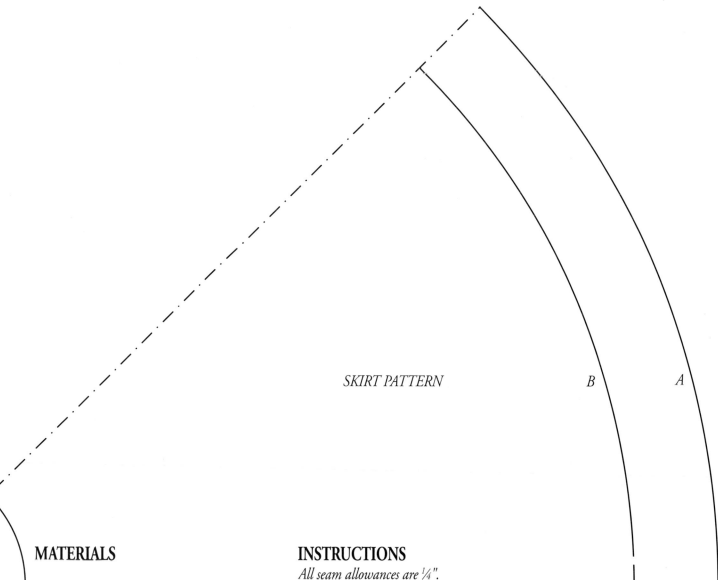

SKIRT PATTERN   B   A

MATERIALS

Completed cross-stitch on periwinkle
    28-count Pastel Linen;
    matching thread
1 yard (45"-wide) red miniprint;
    matching thread
1⅝ yards (⅛") cording
1½ yards (¾"-wide) maroon
    grosgrain ribbon
1½ yards (⅜"-wide) medium blue
    grosgrain ribbon
1½ yards (¼"-wide) white grosgrain
    ribbon; matching thread
4 (½"-wide) white craft stars
Tracing paper
Transparent tape
Dressmaker's pen

INSTRUCTIONS
All seam allowances are ¼".

1. Trace and cut out Skirt Pattern B 8 times. Tape sections together to form circle, leaving first and last unattached for skirt opening. With pattern centered on design piece and open ends of pattern centered along unstitched marked line, trace and cut out. Using same pattern, cut 1 circle from fleece for lining and 1 from miniprint for backing.

2. To make piping, cut 1"-wide bias strips from remaining miniprint, piecing as needed to equal 57". Make corded piping.

3. Baste fleece to wrong side of skirt top. With right sides facing and raw edges aligned, stitch piping along outside edge of top, catching fleece in seam. With right sides facing, raw edges aligned, and piping toward center, stitch skirt top and backing together, leaving open along 1 short edge. Trim corners and turn. Slipstitch opening closed.

4. Cut each ribbon into 4 equal lengths. Handling 1 color of each as 1, tie into a bow. Repeat to make 3 more bows. Referring to photograph, center and tack 1 bow on each side of stitched motifs. Tack 1 star to each bow. Trim ends of ribbons at an angle, varying lengths.

Little Witchie Motif

FABRICS	DESIGN AREAS
11-count	3⅛" x 2⅛"
14-count	2½" x 1¾"
18-count	2" x 1⅜"
22-count	1⅝" x 1⅛"

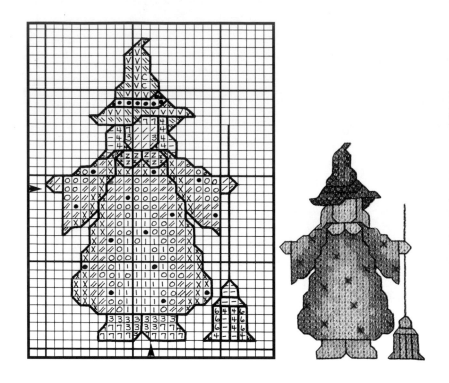

DMC Colors
(used for sample)

Step 1: Cross-stitch (2 strands)

3	3	353	Peach
•		355	Terra Cotta-dk.
6	6	436	Tan
4	4	437	Tan-lt.
X	X	640	Beige Gray-vy. dk.
⁄⁄	⁄⁄	642	Beige Gray-dk.
O	6	644	Beige Gray-med.
\\	\\	645	Beaver Gray-vy. dk.
V	V	646	Beaver Gray-dk.
C	C	647	Beaver Gray-med.
Z	Z	712	Cream
–		738	Tan-vy. lt.
7		754	Peach-lt.
I		822	Beige Gray-lt.
/		948	Peach-vy. lt.

Step 2: Backstitch (1 strand)

	3371	Black Brown

MATERIALS

Completed cross-stitch on ivory 20-count Valerie; matching thread
1 yard (45"-wide) black fabric; matching thread
½ yard polyester fleece
1½ yards (⅛") cording
2⅝ yards (1"-wide) black grosgrain ribbon
2⅝ yards (⅜"-wide) gold grosgrain ribbon
1 yard (¼"-wide) black grosgrain ribbon
Tracing paper
Transparent tape
Dressmaker's pen
Fabric glue

INSTRUCTIONS

All seam allowances are ¼".

1. Refer to Steps 1–4 of Little Patriot, substituting skirt Pattern A for circle and black fabric for backing and piping.

2. Cut 1"-wide black ribbon into 4 equal lengths. Cut ⅜"-wide gold ribbon into 4 (7½") lengths and 4 (12") lengths. Cut ¼"-wide black ribbon into 4 (12") lengths. Referring to photograph, glue 1 (1"-wide) black ribbon on each side of stitched motifs, beginning at outer edge of skirt and folding excess over inside of opening. Glue 1 (7½") gold ribbon in center of each 1"-wide black ribbon. Handling ribbons as 1, tie 1 (12") gold ribbon and 1 (12") black ribbon into a bow. Repeat to make 3 more bows. Referring to photograph, glue each bow at base of ribbon strips. Trim ends at an angle, cutting black ribbons shorter than gold.

Santa Motif

FABRICS	DESIGN AREAS
11-count	5⅛" x 3"
14-count	4" x 2¼"
18-count	3⅛" x 1¾"
22-count	2½" x 1½"

56
32

MATERIALS

Completed cross-stitch on white 25-count Lugana; matching thread
1 yard (45"-wide) holiday stripe fabric; matching thread
1½ yards (⅛") cording
2 yards (⅝"-wide) dark green satin ribbon
2 yards (1"-wide) maroon satin ribbon
Tracing paper
Transparent tape
Dressmaker's pen

INSTRUCTIONS

All seam allowances are ¼".

1. Refer to Steps 1–4 of Little Patriot, substituting Skirt Pattern A for circle and stripe fabric for backing and piping.

DMC Colors
(used for sample)

Step 1: Cross-stitch (2 strands)

•	⁄		White
3		353	Peach
O	⁄	415	Pearl Gray
C	⁄	498	Christmas Red-dk.
*	⁄	500	Blue Green-vy. dk.
⁄	⁄	501	Blue Green-dk.
V	⁄	502	Blue Green
C	⁄	503	Blue Green-med.
7	⁄	754	Peach-lt.
X	⁄	814	Garnet-dk.
⁄	⁄	816	Garnet
	⁄	902	Garnet-vy. dk.
ε	⁄	3371	Black Brown
Z	⁄	002	Balger HL Gold

Step 2: Backstitch (1 strand)

	002 Balger HL Gold (star rays)
	3371 Black Brown (all else)

Step 3: French Knot (2 strands)

●	3371 Black Brown (eyes)

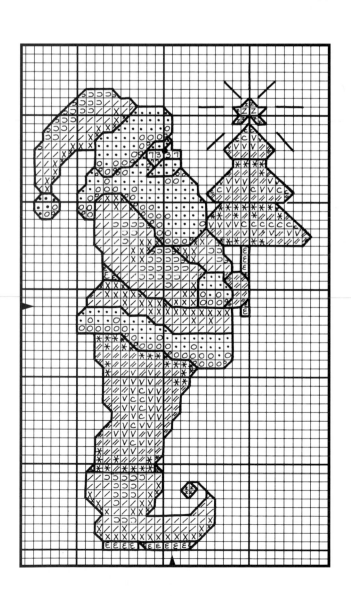

Bunny Motif

FABRICS	DESIGN AREAS
11-count	3⅛" x 4½"
14-count	2⅜" x 3⅝"
18-count	1⅞" x 2¾"
22-count	1½" x 2¼"

DMC Colors
(used for sample)

Step 1: Cross-stitch (2 strands)

•	⁄		White
V	⁄	415	Pearl Gray
*	⁄	518	Wedgwood-lt.
Z	⁄	519	Sky Blue
C	⁄	747	Sky Blue-vy. lt.
\	\	762	Pearl Gray-vy. lt.
r	⁄	776	Pink-med.
/	⁄	818	Baby Pink
–	⁄	819	Baby Pink-lt.

Step 2: Backstitch (1 strand)

	310	Black

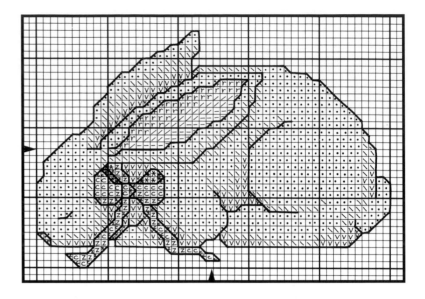

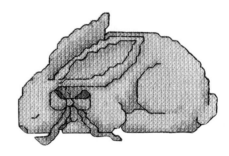

MATERIALS

Completed cross-stitch on carnation 28-count Pastel Linen; matching thread
½ yard (45"-wide) pink fabric; matching thread
½ yard polyester fleece
¼ yard (45"-wide) turquoise satin; matching thread
1½ yards (⅛") cording
1½ yards (¾"-wide) white lace
2⅝ yards (1"-wide) turquoise satin ribbon
Tracing paper
Transparent tape
Dressmaker's pen
Fabric glue

INSTRUCTIONS

All seam allowances are ¼".

1. Refer to Step 1 of Little Patriot, substituting Skirt Pattern A for circle and pink fabric for backing.

2. To make piping, cut 1"-wide bias strips from turquoise satin, piecing as needed to equal 54". Make corded piping.

3. Baste fleece to wrong side of skirt top. With right sides facing and raw edges aligned, baste piping along outside edge of top. Repeat with lace edging. Stitch piping and lace to top, catching fleece in seam.

4. With right sides facing, raw edges aligned, and piping and lace toward center, stitch top and backing together, leaving open along 1 short edge. Trim corners; turn. Slipstitch opening closed.

5. Cut ribbon into 4 (7½") lengths and 4 (16") lengths. Referring to photograph, glue 1 (7½") length on each side of stitched motifs, beginning at outer edge of skirt and folding excess over inside of opening. Tie each 16" length into a bow and glue at base of ribbon strips. Trim ends of ribbons at an angle.

120

I Love You

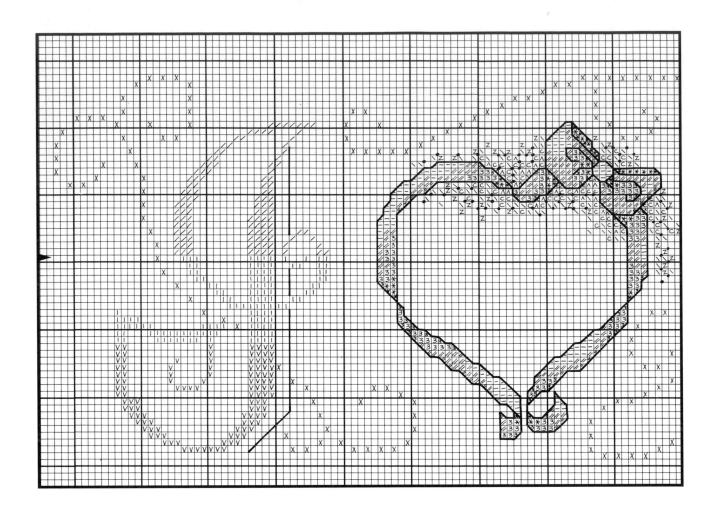

SAMPLE

Sample in photograph was stitched on ivory 28-count Annabelle over 2 threads. Design area is 4½" x 13⅞". Fabric was cut 11" x 20".

FABRICS	DESIGN AREAS
11-count	5¾" x 17⅝"
14-count	4½" x 13⅞"
18-count	3½" x 10¾"
22-count	2⅞" x 8⅞"

DMC Colors
(used for sample)

Step 1: Cross-stitch (2 strands)

ı		223	Shell Pink-med.
/		224	Shell Pink-lt.
*	⁄*	312	Navy Blue-lt.
3	⁄3	322	Navy Blue-vy. lt.
⁄/	⁄	334	Baby Blue-med.
^	⁄^	501	Blue Green-dk.
C	⁄C	502	Blue Green
\	⁄\	503	Blue Green-med.
Z		504	Blue Green-lt.
−	⁄	3325	Baby Blue-lt.
X		3721	Shell Pink-dk.
V		3722	Shell Pink

Step 2: Backstitch (1 strand)

	312 Navy Blue-lt. (bow)
	3721 Shell Pink-dk. (vertical lines)

Step 3: French Knot (2 strands)
(for flowers in greenery)

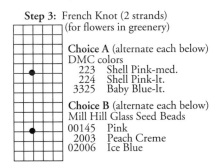

Choice A (alternate each below)
DMC colors
   223   Shell Pink-med.
   224   Shell Pink-lt.
  3325 Baby Blue-lt.

Choice B (alternate each below)
Mill Hill Glass Seed Beads
00145 Pink
 2003 Peach Creme
02006 Ice Blue

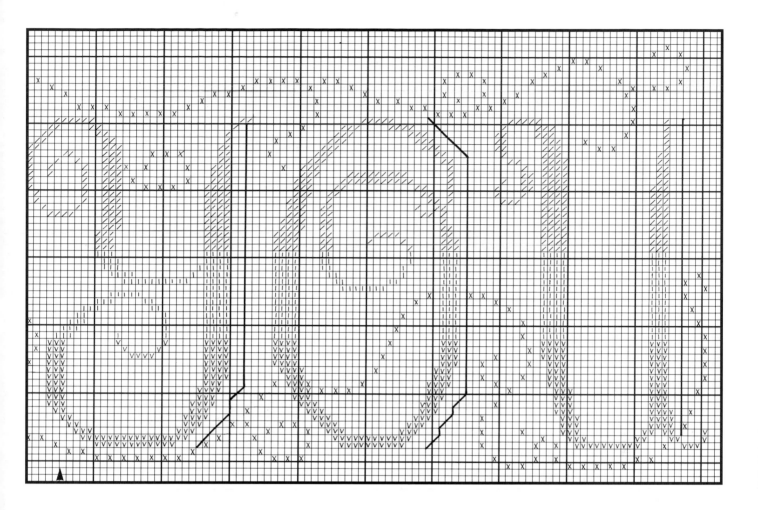

MATERIALS

Completed cross-stitch on ivory
  28-count Annabelle; matching
  thread
¼ yard (45"-wide) cream satin;
  matching thread
1 yard (3½"-wide) pregathered lace
2 yards (⅛"-wide) cream satin
  ribbon, cut in half
1 yard (⅛"-wide) blue satin ribbon
1 yard (⅛"-wide) mauve satin
  ribbon
1 yard prestrung pearl beads
Medium ribbon rosette of desired
  color
Craft glue

INSTRUCTIONS

All seam allowances are ¼".

1. With design centered, trim Annabelle to 6¾" x 16¼". From satin, cut 1 (6¾" x 16¼") piece for pillow back.

2. With right sides facing and gathered edge of lace aligned with raw edges of design piece, pin lace to design piece. Baste lace in place.

3. With right sides facing, raw edges aligned, and lace toward center, stitch pillow front to back, leaving an opening for turning. Trim corners; turn and stuff. Slipstitch opening closed.

4. Handling satin ribbons and prestrung pearl beads as 1, make several 3" loops, leaving 10" tails. Referring to photograph, tack to upper left corner of pillow. Glue rosette to center of bow.

Happy Halloween

SAMPLES

Samples in photograph were stitched on black 22-count Hardanger over 2 threads for Little Pumpkin Pillow and Little Witchie Pillow and on cream 6-count tote over 1 thread for Little Pumpkin Tote. Design areas are 2½" x 2½" for Little Pumpkin Pillow, 3⅛" x 1⅞" for Little Witchie Pillow, and 4⅝" x 4½" for Little Pumpkin Tote. Fabric was cut 9" x 9" for each pillow. Embellish tote with ribbons as desired.

Not So Little Tote was supplied by Janlynn Corporation, 34 Front Street, Indian Orchard, MA 01151.

Little Pumpkin Pillow and Tote Bag

FABRICS	DESIGN AREAS
11-count	2½" x 2½"
14-count	2" x 1⅞"
18-count	1½" x 1½"
22-count	1¼" x 1¼"

Little Witchie Pillow

FABRICS	DESIGN AREAS
11-count	3⅛" x 1⅞"
14-count	2½" x 1½"
18-count	2" x 1⅛"
22-count	1⅞" x 1"

MATERIALS (for 1 pillow)

Completed cross-stitch on black 22-count Hardanger; matching thread
¼ yard (45"-wide) black gingham
¾ yard (⅝"-wide) black satin ribbon, cut in half
Stuffing
Dressmaker's pen

DIRECTIONS

All seam allowances are ¼".

1. With design centered, trim Hardanger to 5½" x 5½" for Little Pumpkin or to 6" x 4½" for Little Witchie. For Little Pumpkin, cut 1 (8½" x 8¾") back piece from gingham; also cut 2 (8¾" x 2") strips and 2 (5½" x 2") strips for border. For Little Witchie, cut 1 (9¼" x 7½") back piece from gingham; also cut 2 (7½" x 2") strips and 2 (6" x 2") strips for border.

2. To make pillow front: Use dressmaker's pen to mark center of 1 long edge of each gingham strip and center of each edge of design piece. With right sides facing, raw edges aligned, and center marks matching, sew short gingham border strips to each side of design piece and then long gingham border strips to top and bottom.

3. With right sides facing and raw edges aligned, stitch pillow front to back, leaving an opening for turning. Trim corners; turn and stuff.

4. Tie each length of ribbon into a bow. Trim ends of ribbons at an angle. Referring to photograph, tack 1 bow to upper left and bottom right corners of pillow.

Little Pumpkin Pillow and Tote Bag

DMC Colors
(used for sample)

Step 1: Cross-stitch (2 strands)

^	⁄	320	Pistachio Green-med.
¢	⁄	367	Pistachio Green-dk.
ı	⁄	368	Pistachio Green-lt.
4		434	Brown-lt.
O	⁄	435	Brown-vy. lt.
−	⁄	436	Tan
V	⁄	744	Yellow-pale
Z	⁄	919	Red Copper
X	⁄	920	Copper-med.
⊃	⁄	921	Copper
⁄	⁄	922	Copper-lt.

Step 2: Backstitch (2 strands)

436	Tan (vine)
3371	Black Brown (all else)

Little Witchie Pillow

DMC Colors
(used for sample)

Step 1: Cross-stitch (2 strands)

⁄	⁄	310	Black
3		353	Peach
●	⁄	355	Terra Cotta-dk.
4	⁄	437	Tan-lt.
X	⁄	640	Beige Gray-vy. dk.
⁄⁄		642	Beige Gray-dk.
O	⁄	644	Beige Gray-med.
\\	⁄	645	Beaver Gray-vy. dk.
V	⁄	646	Beaver Gray-dk.
C	⁄	647	Beaver Gray-med.
Z	⁄	712	Cream
−	⁄	738	Tan-vy. lt.
7		754	Peach-lt.
I		822	Beige Gray-lt.
⁄	⁄	948	Peach-vy. lt.

Step 2: Backstitch (2 strands)

3371	Black Brown

Step 3: French Knot (1 strand)

●	712	Cream (cat's eyes)

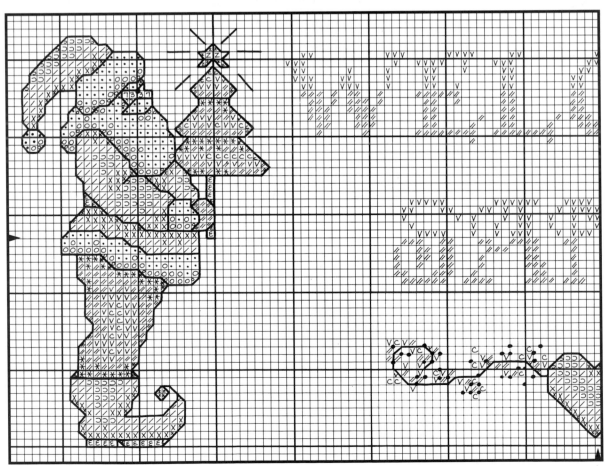

Welcome, Santa

SAMPLE

Sample in phototgraph was stitched on white 25-count Lugana over 2 threads. Design area is 4½" x 12¾". Fabric was cut 11" x 19".

FABRICS	DESIGN AREAS
11-count	5⅛" x 13½"
14-count	4" x 10⅝"
18-count	3⅛" x 8¼"
22-count	2½" x 6¾"

56

149

DMC Colors
(used for sample)

Step 1: Cross-stitch (2 strands)

•	∕		White
3		353	Peach
O	6	415	Pearl Gray
C	8	498	Christmas Red-dk.
*		500	Blue Green-vy. dk.
		501	Blue Green-dk.
V		502	Blue Green
C		503	Blue Green-med.
7	7	754	Peach-lt.
X	x	814	Garnet-dk.
∕	x	816	Garnet
		902	Garnet-vy. dk.
ε	ε	3371	Black Brown
Z	z	002	Balger HL Gold

Step 2: Backstitch (1 strand)

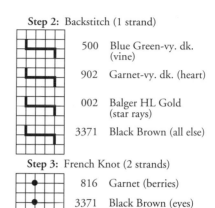

	500	Blue Green-vy. dk. (vine)
	902	Garnet-vy. dk. (heart)
	002	Balger HL Gold (star rays)
	3371	Black Brown (all else)

Step 3: French Knot (2 strands)

•	816	Garnet (berries)
•	3371	Black Brown (eyes)

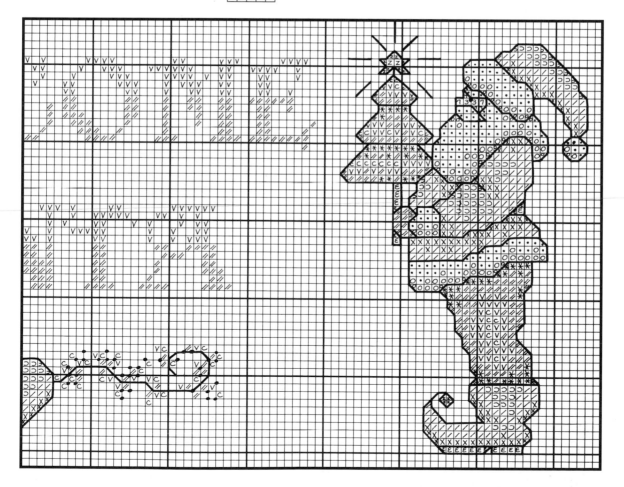

Santa Afghan

SAMPLE

Sample in photograph was stitched on taupe 18-count Anne Cloth afghan over 2 threads. Design area is 13" x 11⅜". Begin stitching center of design in center of afghan.

Afghan (Stock No. 11633) was supplied by Leisure Arts, P.O. Box 5595, Little Rock, AR 72215.

FABRICS	DESIGN AREAS
11-count	10¾" x 9½"
14-count	8⅜" x 7½"
18-count	6½" x 5⅞"
22-count	5⅜" x 4¾"

118
105

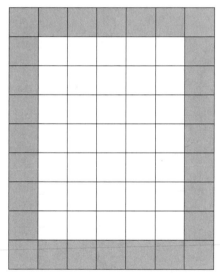

Diagram A

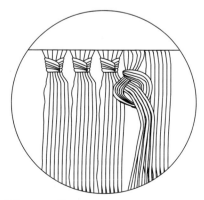

Diagram B

MATERIALS

Completed cross-stitch on taupe 18-count Anne Cloth afghan; matching thread
13⅝ yards (¼"-wide) red satin ribbon
13⅝ yards (¼"-wide) green satin ribbon
Straight pin
Large-eyed needle
4 large jingle bells

INSTRUCTIONS

1. To make fringe, remove selvage and cut afghan to include 7 whole horizontal blocks and 9 whole vertical blocks. Count over 1 complete block and zigzag stitch around entire afghan (see Diagram A). Using straight pin, remove horizontal threads to create fringe. (Finished width measurement should include 5 whole blocks; finished length measurement should include 7 whole blocks.)

2. Beginning at top left corner of afghan, gather 25 threads together and make overhand knot (see Diagram B). Continue clockwise around afghan until you have completed knotting all threads.

3. To make ribbon fringe, cut red and green ribbons into 54 (9") lengths each. Beginning with red in top left corner, use needle to thread 1 length through afghan between 2 fringe knots. Fold length in half and tie ribbon tails in a knot (see photograph). Repeat to add another red ribbon; then add 2 green ribbons. Continue in same manner to alternate 2 ribbons of each color around entire area of afghan.

4. At each corner, thread 1 jingle bell onto afghan fringe below knot and then tie another knot to secure.

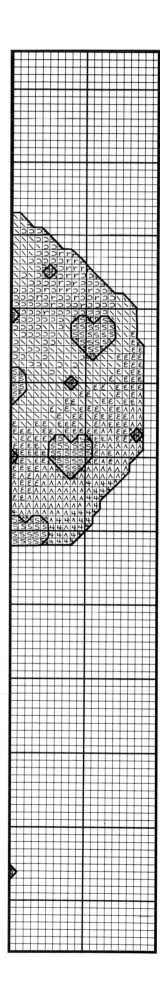

DMC Colors
(used for sample)

Step 1: Cross-stitch (3 strands)

−	∕		White
8	∕8	310	Black
S	∕n	317	Pewter Gray
<	∕<	321	Christmas Red
3	∕3	353	Peach
⋈	∕⋈	413	Pewter Gray-dk.
5	∕5	414	Steel Gray-dk.
P		415	Pearl Gray
4	∕4	433	Brown-med.
∧	∕∧	434	Brown-lt.
ε	∕ε	435	Brown-vy. lt.
⟍	∕⟍	436	Tan
⊃	∕⊃	437	Tan-lt.
∣	∕∣	498	Christmas Red-dk.
⟍⟍	∕⟍⟍	500	Blue Green-vy. dk.
+	∕+	501	Blue Green-dk.
∪	∕∪	502	Blue Green
Z	∕Z	503	Blue Green-med.
⊘	∕⊘	725	Topaz
•	∕•	726	Topaz-lt.
Γ	∕Γ	738	Tan-vy. lt.
∕	∕	746	Off White
7	∕7	754	Peach-lt.
O	∕O	775	Baby Blue-vy. lt.
$	∕$	783	Christmas Gold
L	∕L	796	Royal Blue-dk.
∩	∕∩	797	Royal Blue
N	∕N	798	Delft-dk.
>	∕>	799	Delft-med.
X		815	Garnet-med.
C		816	Garnet
‖	∕‖	820	Royal Blue-vy. dk.
⁄⁄		902	Garnet-vy. dk.
V		3047	Yellow Beige-lt.
R		002	Balger HL Gold
S		080	Balger HL Garnet

Step 2: Backstitch (1 strand)

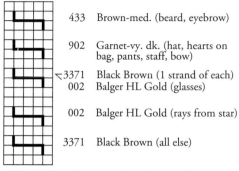

433 Brown-med. (beard, eyebrow)

902 Garnet-vy. dk. (hat, hearts on bag, pants, staff, bow)

3371 Black Brown (1 strand of each)
002 Balger HL Gold (glasses)

002 Balger HL Gold (rays from star)

3371 Black Brown (all else)

Step 3: Long Running Stitch (1 strand)

3371 Black Brown (fringe on scarf)

Christmas Angel Stockings

SAMPLES

Samples in photograph were stitched on white 18-count Tabby Cloth over 2 threads. Design areas are 15⅞" x 11¼" for Girl Angel and 15⅞" x 9½" for Boy Angel. Fabric was cut 22" x 18" for each.

To add date to design, transfer desired numbers from list to graph paper, allowing 1 space between each number. To determine center of date, count total number of spaces and divide by 2. Begin stitching center of date in center of area reserved for date in design.

Girl Angel

FABRICS	DESIGN AREAS
11-count	13" x 9⅛"
14-count	10¼" x 7¼"
18-count	8" x 5⅝"
22-count	6½" x 4⅝"

143 ↑
→ 101

Boy Angel

FABRICS	DESIGN AREAS
11-count	13" x 7¾"
14-count	10¼" x 6⅛"
18-count	8" x 4¾"
22-count	3⅞" x 6½"

143 ↑
→ 85

MATERIALS (for 1 stocking)

Completed cross-stitch on white 18-count Tabby Cloth; matching thread
1 yard (45"-wide) maroon fabric; matching thread
¾ yard (45"-wide) muslin for lining; matching thread
1½ yards (¼") cording
Gold cord with tassel for embellishment (optional)
Tracing paper for pattern
Dressmaker's pen

INSTRUCTIONS

All seam allowances are ¼".

1. Enlarge stocking on grid to make full-size pattern; cut out. Place pattern over stitched design, with top edge of pattern 1¼" above top row of border design and with design centered horizontally; cut out stocking front. From maroon fabric, cut stocking back and 1 (6½" x 5") strip for hanger loop; also cut 1"-wide bias strips, piecing as needed to equal 53". Make corded piping. From muslin, cut 2 stocking pieces.

2. With right sides facing and raw edges aligned, stitch piping around all edges of stocking front. With right sides facing and raw edges aligned, stitch front to back, sewing along stitching line of piping and leaving top edge open. Clip curves and turn.

3. To make hanger loop: With right sides facing and raw edges aligned, fold 6½" x 5" maroon strip in half lengthwise. Stitch long edges together. Fold strip in half to make hanger loop. Referring to photograph, with raw edges aligned and loop toward center, pin loop to right side of stocking back near left seam.

4. To make lining: With right sides facing and raw edges aligned, stitch lining pieces together, leaving top edge open and a large opening in side seam above heel. Clip curves. Do not turn. With right sides facing, slide lining over stocking, matching side seams. Stitch around top edge of stocking, catching ends of hanger loop in seam. Turn stocking through opening in lining. Slipstitch opening closed. Tuck lining inside stocking.

5. Embellish with gold cord with tassel in top left corner, if desired.

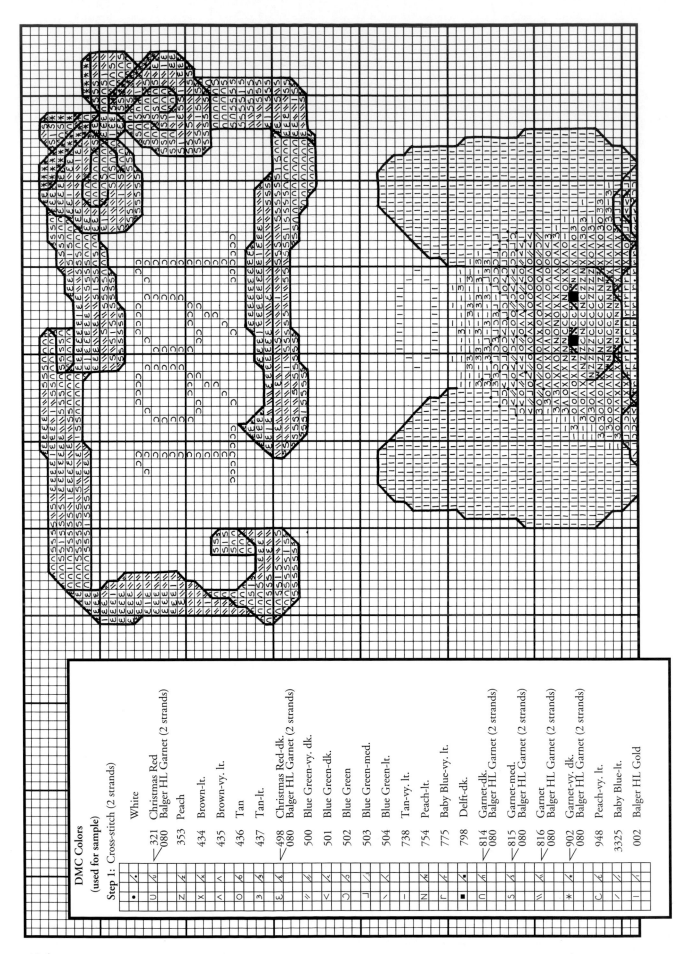

DMC Colors
(used for sample)

Step 1: Cross-stitch (2 strands)

		Color
•		White
U	321 080	Christmas Red / Balger HL Garnet (2 strands)
N	353	Peach
X	434	Brown-lt.
<	435	Brown-vy. lt.
O	436	Tan
3	437	Tan-lt.
ヨ	498 080	Christmas Red-dk. / Balger HL Garnet (2 strands)
V	500	Blue Green-vy. dk.
V	501	Blue Green-dk.
Ɔ	502	Blue Green
Γ	503	Blue Green-med.
✓	504	Blue Green-lt.
I	738	Tan-vy. lt.
N	754	Peach-lt.
r	775	Baby Blue-vy. lt.
■	798	Delft-dk.
∩	814 080	Garnet-dk. / Balger HL Garnet (2 strands)
S	815 080	Garnet-med. / Balger HL Garnet (2 strands)
≡	816 080	Garnet / Balger HL Garnet (2 strands)
*	902 080	Garnet-vy. dk. / Balger HL Garnet (2 strands)
C	948	Peach-vy. lt.
/	3325	Baby Blue-lt.
/	002	Balger HL Gold

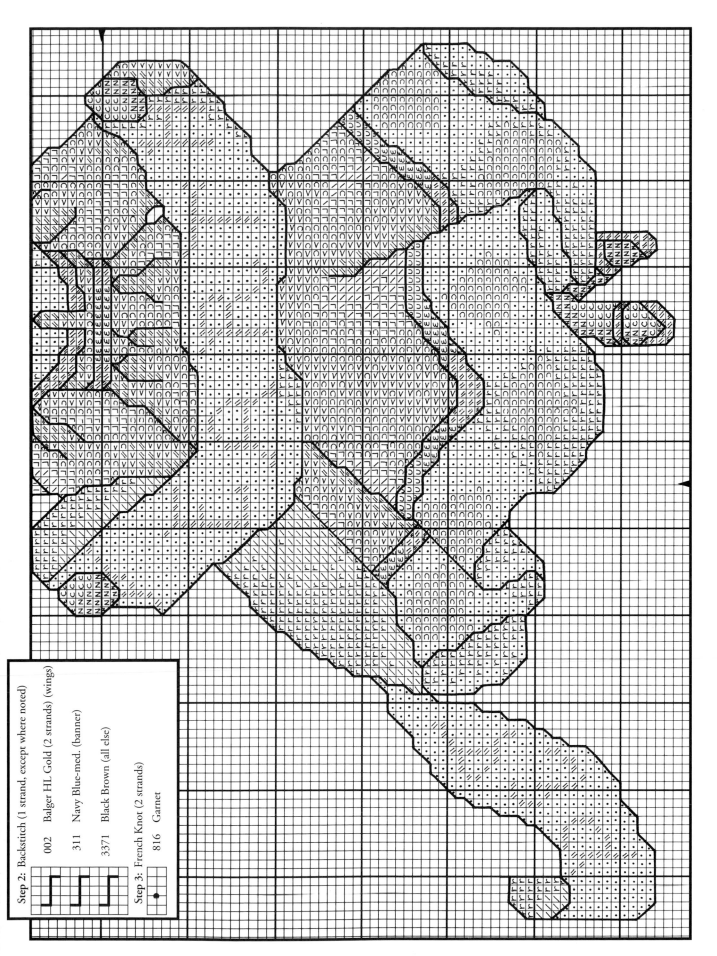

Step 2: Backstitch (1 strand, except where noted)

     002   Balger HL Gold (2 strands) (wings)

     311   Navy Blue-med. (banner)

     3371 Black Brown (all else)

Step 3: French Knot (2 strands)

   •   816   Garnet

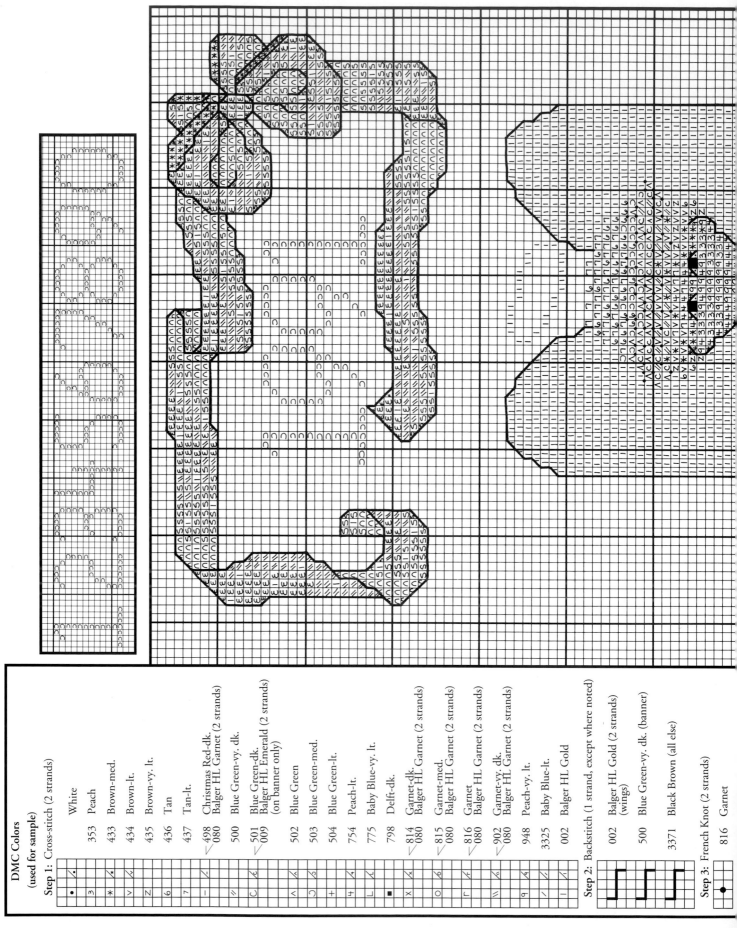

DMC Colors
(used for sample)

Step 1: Cross-stitch (2 strands)

		DMC	Color
•			White
3		353	Peach
*		433	Brown-med.
>		434	Brown-lt.
Z		435	Brown-vy. lt.
6		436	Tan
7		437	Tan-lt.
—	✓	498 / 080	Christmas Red-dk. / Balger HL Garnet (2 strands)
//		500	Blue Green-vy. dk.
C	✓	501 / 009	Blue Green-dk. / Balger HL Emerald (2 strands) (on banner only)
<		502	Blue Green
5		503	Blue Green-med.
+		504	Blue Green-lt.
4		754	Peach-lt.
L		775	Baby Blue-vy. lt.
■		798	Delft-dk.
X	✓	814 / 080	Garnet-dk. / Balger HL Garnet (2 strands)
o		815 / 080	Garnet-med. / Balger HL Garnet (2 strands)
⌐	✓	816 / 080	Garnet / Balger HL Garnet (2 strands)
=	✓	902 / 080	Garnet-vy. dk. / Balger HL Garnet (2 strands)
9		948	Peach-vy. lt.
/		3325	Baby Blue-lt.
‖		002	Balger HL Gold

Step 2: Backstitch (1 strand, except where noted)

002	Balger HL Gold (2 strands) (wings)
500	Blue Green-vy. dk. (banner)
3371	Black Brown (all else)

Step 3: French Knot (2 strands)

●	816	Garnet

136

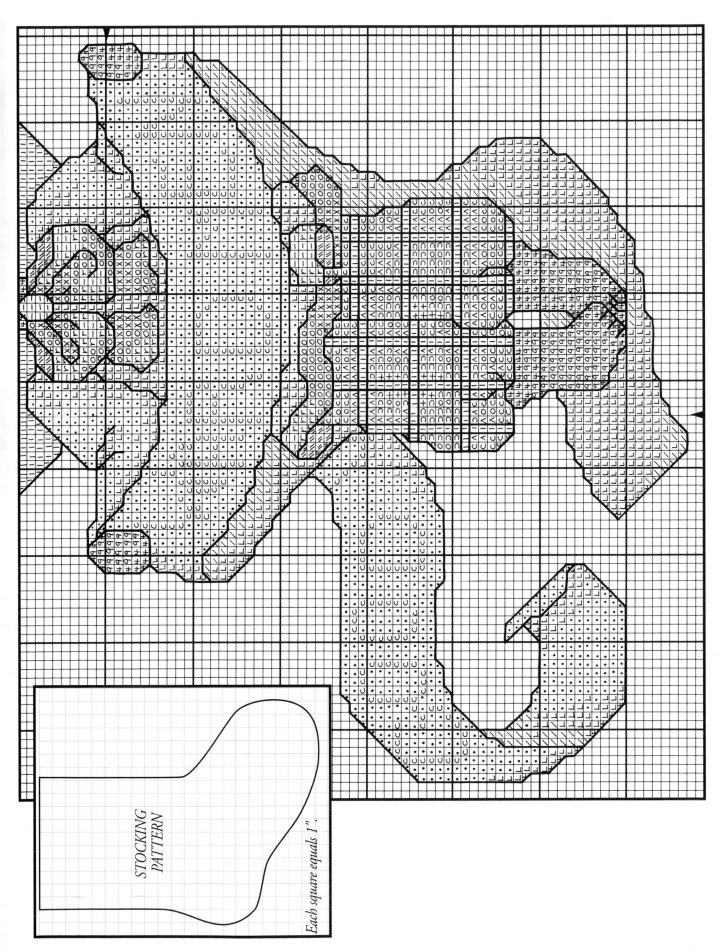

STOCKING PATTERN

Each square equals 1".

137

Holly Table Ensemble

SAMPLES

Samples in photograph were stitched on white 11-count damask Aida over 1 thread for napkins and on white damask tablecloth over 1 thread. Fabric was cut 17½" x 17½" for each napkin.

For napkins, begin stitching motif in lower right corner, 2" from bottom and side edges. For tablecloth, stitch motif in center of each diamond shape.

Bundle of Bows tablecloth (Stock No. 2329-1) was supplied by Zweigart/Joan Toggitt Ltd., Weston Canal Plaza, 2 Riverview Drive, Somerset, NJ 08873.

FABRICS	DESIGN AREAS
11-count	1⅞" x 2⅛"
14-count	1⅜" x 1⅝"
18-count	1⅛" x 1¼"
22-count	⅞" x 1"

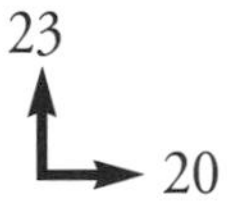

DMC Colors
(used for sample)
Step 1: Cross-stitch (2 strands)

X		319	Pistachio Green-vy. dk.
V		320	Pistachio Green-med.
/		367	Pistachio Green-dk.
\		368	Pistachio Green-lt.
=		498 / 080	Christmas Red-dk. / Balger HL Garnet (2 strands)
^		814 / 080	Garnet-dk. / Balger HL Garnet (2 strands)
O		816 / 080	Garnet / Balger HL Garnet (2 strands)
C		890	Pistachio Green-ultra dk.

Step 2: Backstitch (1 strand)

	890	Pistachio Green-ultra dk. (holly)
	902	Garnet-vy. dk. (berries)

MATERIALS (for 1 napkin)

Completed cross-stitch on white 11-count damask Aida; matching thread
2⅞ yards (1½"-wide) pregathered white lace edging
4⅛ yards (½"-wide) white beading
4⅛ yards (⅛"-wide) dark red satin ribbon
2 yards (⅛"-wide) dark green satin ribbon

INSTRUCTIONS

1. Fold each edge of napkin ¼" to wrong side and stitch.

2. Stitch gathered edge of lace to beading along 1 long edge. Beginning and ending in upper left corner, stitch beading to right side of napkin, overlapping cut edges ½".

3. Beginning and ending in lower right corner, thread red ribbon through beading, leaving 4" tails. Trim excess.

4. Cut green ribbon and remaining red ribbon into 4 (18") lengths each. Handling all lengths as 1, tie into a bow. Using 4" red ribbon tails, tie bow in place.

MATERIALS (for tablecloth)

Completed cross-stitch on white damask tablecloth; matching thread
5 yards (1½"-wide) pregathered white lace edging
5 yards (¾"-wide) white beading
5 yards (5"-wide) white lace edging
17⅞ yards (⅛"-wide) dark red satin ribbon
10⅔ yards (⅛"-wide) dark green satin ribbon

INSTRUCTIONS

1. Tack gathered edge of 1½"-wide lace to 1 edge of beading; tack 5"-wide lace to remaining edge, forming 1 wide strip. With 1½"-wide lace toward center, stitch beading to right side of tablecloth, beginning and ending in 1 corner. Trim excess, if necessary, and overlap cut edges ½".

2. Thread red ribbon through beading along 1 side, leaving 12" tails at each corner and trimming excess. Repeat with remaining sides.

3. Cut green ribbon and remaining red ribbon into 16 (24") lengths each. Separate ribbons into 4 sets, with each set containing 4 lengths of each color. Handling all lengths as 1, tie 1 set of ribbons into a bow. Repeat with remaining sets to make 3 bows. Using 12" red ribbon tails, tie 1 bow in place at each corner.

Christmas Collar

❈ ─────────

SAMPLE

Sample in photograph was stitched on white 28-count Annabelle over 2 threads. Design area is 1⅝" x 2". Fabric for collar was cut 15" x 13". Begin stitching in lower right corner, 2" from bottom edge and 1" from right edge of fabric.

FABRICS	DESIGN AREAS
11-count	1⅞" x 2½"
14-count	1⅜" x 1⅞"
18-count	1⅛" x 1½"
22-count	⅞" x 1¼"

20

27

DMC Colors
(used for sample)

Step 1: Cross-stitch (2 strands)

X	⌐	317	Pewter Gray
C	⌐	318	Steel Gray-lt.
<	⌐	319	Pistachio Green-vy. dk.
3	⌐	321	Christmas Red
7	⌐	367	Pistachio Green-dk.
∧	⌐	414	Steel Gray-dk.
/	⌐	415	Pearl Gray
V	⌐	498	Christmas Red-dk.
•	⌐	762	Pearl Gray-vy. lt.
⫽	⌐	815	Garnet-med.
Z	⌐	818	Baby Pink
\\	⌐	890	Pistachio Green-ultra dk.
*	⌐	902	Garnet-vy. dk.
◢		3371	Black Brown

Step 2: Backstitch (1 strand)

⌐	3371	Black Brown

MATERIALS

Completed cross-stitch on white 28-count Annabelle; matching thread
2¼ yards (⅛"-wide) red satin ribbon, cut in fourths
Double-sided fusible web
Straight pin
Sharp needle
Dressmaker's pen

INSTRUCTIONS

1. To make fringe, use dressmaker's pen to draw line ½" from each edge of Annabelle. Stitch along marked line with close zigzag stitches. Cut fabric up to zigzag stitches at 2½" intervals. Using a straight pin, pull away horizontal threads to create fringe.

2. To make collar front and back, fold fabric in half widthwise, mark center, and cut fabric in half along marked line. Cut 2 (1" x 12") strips of fusible web. Fold top edges of collar front and back 1" to wrong side. For each piece, place fusible web between layers at fold and, following manufacturer's instructions, fuse top edges in place.

3. For ribbon ties, fold each length in half. Along top edge of collar front, use a sharp needle to make a small hole in fabric 1¾" from each side. Repeat with collar back.

4. Thread doubled end of 1 ribbon through 1 hole, slip cut ends of ribbon through loop, and pull tightly. Repeat with remaining ribbons and holes. Trim ends of ribbons at an angle.

5. Referring to photograph, join collar front to back by tying ribbons into bows at shoulders, adjusting to fit as necessary.

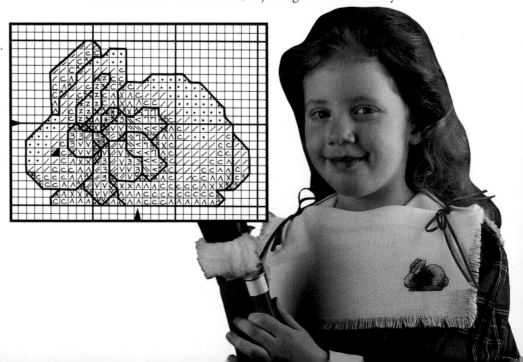

GENERAL INSTRUCTIONS

PREPARATION

Design Area: To determine area of a design stitched over one thread, divide stitch count of design by thread count of fabric. If design is stitched over two threads, divide stitch count by one-half of thread count. In designations of design areas, vertical measurements are given first, horizontal measurements second.

Fabrics: Most designs in this book were stitched on even-weave fabrics made especially for cross-stitch. In sample paragraphs, fabrics are identified by color, thread count, and name. If your local needlework shop does not stock a particular fabric, see Suppliers for ordering information.

Floss: Designs in this book call for DMC six-strand embroidery floss. (A few designs also use Balger metallic threads.) Cut floss into 18" lengths; separate strands; then recombine and thread needle with number of strands called for in color codes.

Graphs and Color Codes: In graphs, a square containing a symbol represents one stitch to be worked on fabric. Each symbol corresponds to a specific color of DMC floss, identified by number and name in color code. Stitches other than cross-stitch, such as backstitch and French knots, are also represented in both graphs and color codes.

Stitch Count: Stitch count equals number of stitches in design, counted both vertically and horizontally, as indicated by arrows whose bases are joined in a right angle.

Thread Count: Thread count equals number of parallel threads per inch in weave of fabric. Thus, 14-count fabric has 14 threads per inch, 18-count fabric has 18 threads per inch, and so on.

GETTING STARTED

Hoop or Frame: Using an embroidery hoop or frame to keep fabric taut makes it easier to form uniform stitches. Select a hoop or frame large enough to accommodate entire design. Place screw or clamp of hoop in a 10 o'clock position (or 2 o'clock, if you are left-handed) to keep it from catching floss.

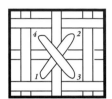

Diagram A

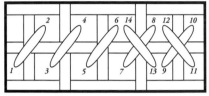

Diagram B

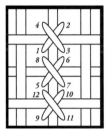

Diagram C

Diagram D

Diagram E

Needles: To avoid splitting fabric threads, use a blunt tapestry needle. With fabric that has 11 or fewer threads per inch, use a size-24 needle. With fabric that has 14 threads per inch, use a size-24 or 26 needle. With fabric that has 16 or more threads per inch, use a size-26 needle.

Preparing Fabric: Cut fabric at least 3" larger on all sides than design area. To keep edges of fabric from fraying while you work on design, whipstitch or machine-zigzag raw edges or apply liquid ravel preventer and allow to dry.

Centering Design: To make sure that completed design is centered on fabric, use the following procedure: First, fold fabric into quarters, folding from left to right and then from top to bottom. Intersection of folds is center of fabric. To find center of design, follow lines indicated by arrows at edges of graph until lines intersect. If there is a symbol at center of design, begin stitching there. If there is no symbol at center of design, calculate distance from center of design to nearest symbol and begin stitching there.

Securing Floss: Bring needle and most of floss up through fabric, holding a 1" tail of floss behind fabric where first stitches will be taken. Work first four or five stitches over tail of floss to secure it.

You can also use waste knot method. After tying a knot at end of floss, bring needle down through fabric about 1" from where first stitch will be taken. Plan placement of waste knot so that first four or five stitches will cover and secure 1" of floss on back of fabric, as described above. After floss has been secured, cut off knot.

To secure floss when finished, run needle and floss under four or five stitches on back of design and trim tail close to fabric. Subsequent lengths of floss may be secured in same manner.

STITCHES

Cross-stitch: When a symbol takes up an entire square on graph, make one complete cross-stitch. Bring needle and floss up at 1, down at 2, up again at 3, and down at 4 (see Diagram A).

For horizontal rows, work understitches in one journey, moving from left to right; then work overstitches in a second journey, moving from right to left (see Diagram B). For vertical rows, complete each stitch individually (see Diagram C). All stitches should lie in same direction—that is, all understitches must slant in same direction and all overstitches must slant in opposite direction.

When a symbol fills only half of a square on graph, make a three-quarter stitch (see Diagram D). This creates a curved line in design. If you are working over one thread, short understitch will pierce fabric thread; if you are working over two threads, understitch will go down in hole between two threads. In each case long stitch is overstitch,

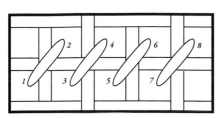

Diagram F

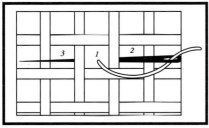

Diagram G

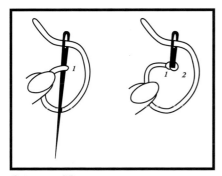

Diagram H

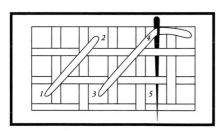

Diagram I

even though this may violate rule that all stitches should lie in same direction.

When two symbols occupy a single square on graph, make a three-quarter stitch and a quarter stitch to fill square. Which symbol applies to which stitch depends on line you want to emphasize—use three-quarter stitch to express dominant line or color (see Diagram E).

Half-cross: Sometimes part of a design calls for only the first half of a cross-stitch, or understitch, to be worked. Called a half-cross, this stitch is represented by its own symbol and step in color code (see Diagram F).

Backstitch: Bring needle and floss up at 1, down at 2, and up again at 3. Going back down at 1, continue stitching in same manner (see Diagram G).

French Knots: Bring needle and floss up at 1. Wrap floss once around needle and insert needle at 2, holding floss taut so that knot remains close to needle. Bring needle and floss down through fabric at 2, holding floss until it must be released (see Diagram H).

Long Running Stitch: Long running stitches are represented in graphs and color codes by continuous heavy black lines.

WORKING DESIGN

Keeping Design Clean: Always wash your hands well and avoid using hand creams and lotions before you begin stitching. As each section is stitched, fold or roll fabric so that front of embroidery faces inward.

Working over One Fabric Thread: For smooth, even stitches, use the push-and-pull method when working over one thread. Push needle straight up through fabric and pull floss completely through to front of fabric. To bring needle to back again, push needle straight down and pull needle and floss completely through to back.

Working over Two Fabric Threads: Some experts recommend using the push-and-pull method (see above) for working over either one or two threads, while others suggest the sewing method for working over two threads. To use sewing method, first push needle straight up through fabric at 1. Then insert needle at 2 from front of fabric. Guide tip of needle to back of fabric and then to front at 3 in one motion; pull needle and floss through fabric, keeping your stitching hand in front of fabric at all times (see Diagram I).

Carrying Floss: To carry floss, weave it under previously worked stitches on back. Never carry floss across fabric that is not or will not be stitched. Carried threads, especially dark ones, will show through openings in fabric.

Untwisting Floss: Cut floss no longer than 18", because longer lengths tend to twist and knot during stitching; floss covers best when lying flat against fabric. If floss becomes twisted, suspend your needle and allow floss to unwind.

FINISHING UP

Signing and Dating Work: Always sign and date your work to enrich its meaning for future generations. Using a neutral color of floss, backstitch or cross-stitch your name or initials and year in lower right-hand corner.

Cleaning Work: Soak work in cold water with a mild liquid soap, such as Joy or Dawn, for about 5 to 10 minutes. Rinse thoroughly under running water. Roll work in a towel to remove excess water; do not wring. Place face down on a dry towel and, with iron on warm setting, press until dry.

Suppliers

Zweigart Fabrics:
Zweigart/Joan Toggitt, Ltd.,
Weston Canal Plaza, 2 Riverview
Drive, Somerset, NJ 08873
White 11-count Damask Aida
Ivory 14-count Aida
Lavender 18-count Davosa
Cream 18-count Tabby Cloth
White 18-count Tabby Cloth
Cream 19-count Cork Linen
White 19-count Cork Linen
White 20-count Ariosa
Ivory 20-count Valerie
Black 22-count Hardanger
White 25-count Lugana
Carnation 28-count Pastel Linen
Cream 28-count Pastel Linen
Daffodil 28-count Pastel Linen
Periwinkle 28-count Pastel Linen

Pistachio 28-count Pastel Linen
Ice Blue 28-count Annabelle
Ivory 28-count Annabelle
White 28-count Annabelle
Ivory 28-count Jubilee
Natural 28-count Linen
Tea-dyed 28-count Linen
White 28-count Quaker Cloth
White Damask Bundle of Bows
  Tablecloth

Wichelt Fabrics:
Wichelt Imports, Rural Route 1,
Stoddard, WI 54658
White 14-count Astoria
White 20-count Irish Linen

Leisure Arts Fabrics:
Leisure Arts, P.O. Box 5595,

Little Rock, AR 72215
Soft White 18-count Anne Cloth
Taupe 18-count Anne Cloth

Cross My Heart Fabrics:
Cross My Heart, Inc., 4725
Commercial Drive, Huntsville,
AL 35816
Camel 18-count Highland
Natural 19-count Highland

Mill Hill Beads
Gay Bowles Sales, Inc., 1310
Plainfield Avenue, Janesville,
WI 53547

Balger Products
Kreinik Mfg. Co., Inc., P.O. Box
1966, Parkersburg, WV 26102